# Threads of Iron

*Selected previous publications by Andrew Duncan*

Poetry

*In a German Hotel*
*Cut Memories and False Commands*
*Sound Surface*
*Alien Skies*
*Switching and Main Exchange**
*Pauper Estate**
*Anxiety before Entering a Room. New and selected poems*
*Surveillance and Compliance*
*Skeleton Looking at Chinese Pictures*
*The Imaginary in Geometry*
*Savage Survivals (amid modern suavity)**
*In Five Eyes**

Criticism

*The Poetry Scene in the Nineties* (internet only)
*Centre and Periphery in Modern British Poetry*
*The Failure of Conservatism in Modern British Poetry*
*Origins of the Underground*
*The Council of Heresy**
*The Long 1950s**
*Fulfilling the Silent Rules* (forthcoming)

As editor

*Don't Stop Me Talking* (with Tim Allen)
*Angel Exhaust* (magazine: 1992–98 and 2005–   )
Joseph Macleod: *Cyclic Serial Zeniths from the Flux*

*Shearsman titles

# Threads of Iron

Andrew Duncan

Shearsman Books

First published in the United Kingdom in 2013 by
Shearsman Books
50 Westons Hill Drive
Emersons Green
BRISTOL
BS16 7DF

Shearsman Books Ltd Registered Office
30–31 St. James Place, Mangotsfield, Bristol BS16 9JB
(this address not for correspondence)

www.shearsman.com

ISBN 978-1-84861-289-1

Copyright © Andrew Duncan, 1991, 2000, 2003, 2013.

The right of Andrew Duncan to be identified as the author
of this work has been asserted by him in accordance with the
Copyrights, Designs and Patents Act of 1988.
All rights reserved.

My thanks for earlier publication of parts of this book by
John Wilkinson and Rod Mengham, Tim Longville,
James Lasdun and Robin Robertson, Peter Riley,
Ken Edwards, Chris Hamilton-Emery.

Part of this volume originally appeared in
*Cut Memories & False Commands* (London: Reality Street Editions, 1991)
and the rest appeared in *Switching and Main Exchange*
(Kentisbeare: Shearsman Books, 2000).

# Contents

| | |
|---|---|
| Author's Note | 7 |
| | |
| Endless Highway (ametrical foreword) | 11 |
| A House on the Endless Highway | 15 |
| White Block | 19 |
| A Flock of Deer by Moonlight | 21 |
| In My Time of Dying | 26 |
| Sympathetic | 30 |
| Sickle Moon | 31 |
| Heavy Wind | 32 |
| Circulation | 33 |
| Photo Flakes Falling | 35 |
| The Winnowing | 36 |
| Black Pane and Decor | 38 |
| Words Versus Buildings | 47 |
| Perfect Skin | 51 |
| Heavy Metal | 53 |
| Literacy | 55 |
| Flight | 59 |
| Flayed Inside | 60 |
| Tamur Jan | 61 |
| Piccadilly Saturday Night | 63 |
| L'Algérie, c'est la France | 65 |
| Passover | 67 |
| Falkenhain | 68 |
| Nationality | 77 |
| For John Riley | 80 |
| Deutsche Industrienorm | 82 |
| Yellow Ice, Enfield | 90 |
| Rats and Monkeys | 92 |
| Machina Carnis | 94 |
| Visitors to Art Galleries Considered as one of the Fine Arts | 95 |
| Fen Landscape | 98 |
| Interview with the Spirit of the Age | 100 |

| | |
|---|---|
| Almond Wind | 102 |
| For an Artist, Having Died in his Dreams | 105 |
| *In memoriam* Pablo Neruda | 109 |
| On First Publication | 113 |
| The Academy | 114 |
| Trotsky from Petrograd | 115 |
| Office Boy | 117 |
| Oreads | 119 |
| In Charnwood | 123 |
| Schönheit Schönheit | 125 |
| Dhofar | 127 |
| Turkish Music | 129 |
| Builders in Winter | 135 |
| British Steel | 137 |
| Britanskaya SSR | 140 |
| Lusitanian Angel | 143 |
| 'Laughing Man', Self-Portrait by Richard Gerstl | 147 |
| Engineer Grade II | 149 |
| In the Red Grove | 153 |
| The Poet and the Schizophrenic | 156 |
| Dead Wind | 158 |

# Author's Note

A comment on time sequence to avoid confusion. I wrote a group of poems, in 1980-1, called *Threads of Iron*. For format reasons the book was divided. Part came out as a book in 1991 (*Cut Memories and False Commands*) and the rest in 2000 (*Switching and Main Exchange*). They are now put together for the first time. The poems are not all related to each other except that they came out of the situation of one person in one stretch of time. They are designed to complement each other. They are presented in the form that they reached slightly later, around 1986, when Paladin were interested in the book for their poetry series (about to be discontinued).

*Threads of Iron*

# Endless Highway

I am writing this in a room above the North Circular. From here I shuttle to and from work each day, like a chicken on a wire. From this dead point, this well full of earth and leavings, I watch the city spread out like the dead forms of my depression.

Like an iron chain the cars go by; now and then there is a break where flesh can slip past, thought grit and fumes rise up like a wall. The cars are like the moving chain of sordid and inevitable thoughts, which I try to breach by whatever methods. The membrane of my senses seems to me like a wall—the channel of my thoughts itself like a North Circular—the churning of my body and my unconscious themselves like a factory. Here motion itself is stasis.

I despair of all the inhabitants of this city. Insomuch, I can express my emotions without fear of being understood. If I infringe this loneliness, its immurements and starvations, what symmetrical devastation will I find? what stain upon the adamic diagram of perfection, of ability to struggle? How could I sustain two such anguishes as my own? I wrote this to help a few people who were beyond my help. I cut abstract patterns out of anxiety and other people and construct the future with them.

I came here out of a darkness I can't describe. My emotional memories are my accusation. My rationality is prescribed by the firm's; it is only in the lapses that I can grasp my own being at all: in the bright midnight, in seizures of passion, in the rusty mirrors of a violent despair, in the voices of error. I hate figures, symbols, words, thoughts, instructions, orders; for me symbols are my daily bread. Culture is the education of a bureaucrat. Already words differ from sensation as bureaucracy differs from goods and labour. We who once filled clay tablets with the tallies of Temple goods and Pharaoh's goods, creating a tiny city of mud and reeds, now feed computers with strings of data: at the call of a Power which holds dominion over all signs. Ideogram city, scorpion city! At night I process more strings of data: the clerk's equivalent of muscle cramps.

Manpower efficiency records: here is reality in all its mediocrity, its pointless master of technique, its absence of nature, its monopoly of profits and control in an electric leash, in the name of a mechanization which alienation can name but not reverse. Economics: astronomy broken down to granules of irresistible force, nativity or noon-points marked on the earth; tides dispersing the constellations of the brain, its feeble pulses and signs; overwhelming the weaker signal. A surgeon deftly setting up prisons of conditioning. Understand. Try not to forget.

Every day I see the workforce, like animals in a cage, like ruined hovels propped up, like liquid buds deformed by an unknown force. What is disgusting except Man? Even repulsion is a door, like the memory of something better. Are they hypocrites? or is the source of desire lost for ever? abandoned to the greater force of Submission? I do not write from security or knowledge. I am dust in the endless eye. As soon as I realize that I am like them the pain will stop and my life will start again as a conformist, a model prisoner who knows that every outburst hurts the group and makes the petty gratifications dry up. All day I drink in the factory and at night I vomit it out: I am empty, purged, total. Nothing I think is true. When rhythmic terror forces arrogance to tear down its silence, for a few moments I breathe, I experience, I speak in black metric jags and high flawless walls. Despair is my only claim to adequacy; but in that narrow and empty space, there will be no beauty which is not the reflection of what it conceals. Flowers flatter Nature, as the despondent relatives try to console the mad by painting their faces; palaces have swarms of poor labourers pinned out on them like Christ on his steelyard; in the luxury hotels, the work is done by Turks who sleep in damp rooms and are afraid of the police. I practise hypocrisy but when wires are torn out the brain no longer registers images or cleans itself. I try to cut out the live points of my eye like someone wiping off digits on a perspex screen.

I know what beauty is; I have nothing to call beautiful; I only know the indifference of the masses to poetic experience; only a few fragments of such beauty as to rear up a building from its ruins; I say, poems are like the hymns which children sing in unease and vacuity, laid out in rows and watched with malice by an instructor. Poetry shines, on these tumbled bricks and purple-fungal seeps, like a few sparks of sweet water. The poetic tradition transmitted a superiority without stalk or motive, an inexclusive heritage of estates; already it's clear that the sensation of power rested entirely on the memory of class oppression. In fine rooms, we waited discreetly like servants; using fine words to discuss the feats and frolics of noble persons. Poetry is in shock at the death of the aristocracy and of a grandiose Church. I can't find work as a ritualist or a recorder of Court life. For those who are not free of the real pressure of earthly objects, fluency of words is a mockery. One sees the purity of Nature only because he has does not have to teach it, nor to stoop to hoe it; pure, this symbol is empty, the gaze which fixes it is jerky and superficial. It is the gaze of anxiety which is full of thriving images, and it is these half-forms which I must seek to slow down, discern, transmute.

The claw of the raptor seeks to shape the mental flux to something firm: the ball of its clutch. This imperious identification is itself something fragile, as the identity repeatedly reverses, and chooses the soiled objects, the worn the failed the inferior, to pull into itself. There are more rabbits than kestrels. The truly weak are not raised by the aggression of the artist; the rhythmic onslaught weakens their own voice; identifying already calls for too much strength. My dream palaces mock those who hear voices coming from behind the walls. I neither helped the weak nor helped myself, incarnating a firm voice I heard calling out from behind the sodium-yellow walls of night.

When I close my eyes, I can see the City laid out like a huge scorpion of partitions and restrictions; every image I dredge up from the stellar furnace of shapes is laid out on this grid of fear and dispossession. I think the same image is stamped on each brick as on the whole City and on each cell of my thoughts.

I think, if I found the right geometry (a suite of shears and distortions), the City itself would rotate into a truly significant shape, a frieze of pure and forceful images. Could this be the true setting-out of my desires, my emotions; could this be the dynamic portrait of the human soul? Eight million people wander in these grids as if in the archives of dead memory. See, here we have the solidity of infinite complexes of despair, 20,000 streets under a narrow sky and 20,000 days under a weight harsh as metal. I wander the streets of illusory cities, Heliopolis, Babylon, Tenochtitlán, Caer Ys, Second London; I imagine factories of liberated power and liberated bodies, classically tensed in the collective task. I plunge my hand in the unnameable. I cut through a membrane in my head to let the shapes of error pour through in a gush of ionized metals, of molten limbs. Everything passes across that membrane: empires, languages, revolutions, economies; a lexicon of desires and implements. I daze myself with languages I hardly know. I run through the Museum and let its objects rush through my eyes like mountains rushing past a train. I pour data into my head like a man pouring brandy into a bottle. Wild forces lance by like birds along great meridians of air. Oracular winds blow.

Sensations move by on bands of irreversible monotony, mechanical destructive commands to obsolete executor systems, words blocked in the scanning lapses of syntax. For the melancholic, the thought of happiness cannot be thought: this too is part of syntax, sensations pinned under dead blocks, as if a flight of arrows defeated by gravity. I'm a living sickness, objects become deformed as they enter my senses; I create a second world by shearing the coordinates of the first one, and the second is a caricature, a figure of fun. I sift through a roomful of photographs, trying to pin down what's wrong.

The buildings in which we were unhappy are falling apart, frittered by the nagging of molar Time. Every day we labour to reconstruct the world to the old drawings, sweating to tug the last centimetre into place and let it vanish in the imperceptibility of repetition; but it changes anyway. The salts of corpses migrate in the earth, upon which the civil order slides through unimaginable horizons of decay to fall at last.

Someone else is in this room. You can tell by the curtain stirring-the stain in the wine glass-the papers rustling on the table. My breath catches in the attempt to synchronise, and a face just refrains from shaving itself with my hand. I feel my shape flowing off its frame, liquidated, humiliated, as a radiant body image inflicts itself on my sparse and sallow flesh. In the mirror, my bones break through my skin, grey fat tears off my face, the image peels off my pupil and splinters. Rhythms start up out of the air-china shakes on a tray-the tones of the walls shift slightly. The words in my books change. Red pointing appears in the Bible; I hold it up to the light and a new text emerges. Reading by the broken silver of the moon, I start to recite it.

## A House on the Endless Highway

The house which furbishes images like skins
The house in which texts
Clings to the ceilings and partitions
Like bats or winter butterflies
The house where lies drip off the eaves

The house in which the rooms dream
In which people's images are dismantled behind closed doors
And mirrors hide distorted faces
Where the wardrobes are full of old clothes, dissolved bodies
The house where each gaze rejects what it sees
The house near the Greek Church
The house near the New River
The house near the Jehovah's Witnesses' hall
The house near the Pentecostals
The house on the Endless Highway

The house ruined by fantasies, the inexistent house
The house whose outline is denied by music
The house made of dead skin, a shell
Of ragged flesh, seethed
Into tatters of grey leather, heated up
Too many times: the brew of a shared table.

The house of debris years old
The house of compacted filth

The house
Where Helena is happy in the afternoon
To be drunk and feel the evening coming
But takes valium so she can cook her old man's dinner
And do housework for one room, three people.
Night brings the family together,
The feeling stretches out from the window to the wall.
The light is dim, the room replaced by music,

Its every line effaced by blue smoke
So you kick your child lying sleeping on the floor
And he wakes and cries.

The camera eye sweeps from wall to wall
It's a slum it's a room
It's a cave a hearth a flame
It's a being
It's the frame defining events
It's a forest, a green dell, a silver screen
It's a room it's a home
It's a childhood

The house of the Drunken Sages
The house of the Ascetics who refrain from thought
The house
To whose geometry we are adapted

The house where there is an ageing man
I see by day
With a doddering step and a vague expression
In a dirty lab coat testing printed circuits
In the factory down the road,
In a dingy humming corridor.
He sits alone in an upper room
Listening to the police frequencies.
A family? that's like a second job.
The bright parts of machinery
Replace the body and its personality, turned low.
He observes unseen
In the room full of alien words,
Motorway stories.

In the front room where the traffic noise
Soaks the air like water, the two gays,
Back from the BR line gang,
Clinging to the rim of the motorway

Shout at each other lively with rage;
Where every anguish is reduced to words
And pure freedom is the power
Of causing somebody pain; the surface
Of the loved object is shredded and smeared and gouged.
They drink so as to tell the truth without blocks
And the truth is just a wish
And the wish is to wipe somebody out.
The cordon of loathing which extends between us populates
The house, as lying versions of each of us
Are tortured in slight slow fictions in the next room
And rebroadcast to become the strings of consciousness,
The words that push through the sill. Jammed frequencies.
Other people's lies constitute a household.
At four am I lie awake
Waiting for work
Listening to the men shouting in the next room
And seeing my curse already come true.

The house
For those who can't afford a home
For those who can't afford a family
To crawl at the end of the day
Shut the door
And think about doing a more difficult job.
The house where motion is replaced by the traffic.
The house where we count from one to a thousand
And from a thousand down to zero.
The house where I span out four years.

The house where each morning
My shaking hand shaves tatters off my face
The blood flows in the heart of the mirror
And I haul on a rope of empty spaces

I sit up in my room

The room where I stage my artistic triumphs
The room like a mouth reciting us as lies
The room of unrequited love, the empty
Space where I talk about want and am found
Wanting. I talk about literature, she talks about
Property. I live alone in a paper house.
I hang a thousand paintings in the house
And each day I change one detail.
The devices unfold forever.
I talk and talk. It's like someone coughing.
Whatever is not the case
Is what I fill the room with.

## White Block

I cross the bridge into the white block
The train jumps straight as a shell
The train wails like a lost cry
Bent by velocity.
Under the eye which empties all it sees
I drift in the sea of numbers.
My eye crosses to the opposite blank façade
And sees another blank eye staring out at me.
My gaze skips up the ornamentless cliff of windows,
Paranoid architecture,
Three thousand gasps of dead light,
And casts on off-white my next three thousand days.

Three thousand frames of arrested motion.
I watch myself as if from a great distance.
Rifts open in the wall,
I try to close them.
A green flash shoots across the building
Fleeting
A flaw in my brain.

I look at the pictures of memory.
The mechanism is broken, the recurrence
Caught in its onset.
My limbs at night are untwisted, slack.
I could be ten thousand people just like me.
In the morning, whose body wakes up?
This fool? this unstrung flesh?

Probing each crack in the flags of the White Block,
I go over my nerves until my fingers bleed
But cannot find the spark whose track I saw
In the firmament.

I put microphones into the walls and floors.
A micro pickup pocked into the bone
Sends back miles of textural noise,
A gigantic slow shudder, an Atlantic surf.
I play the tape in the hope that years will pass.
I subtend tangents and freeze out clusters,
I draw the arcs of the White Block.

I shred and shred
The images of the past
But nothing moves, no pattern rises.
I tear skin from skin
I tear face from face
I tear thread from thread
There is no sustenance.

A white shadow flits along the wall and the train wails
The cry which metal tears from metal
In the mutilation dirge of its parting
And the greenness of its velocity
Like a street singer howling a murder ballad
And like the lost voice of this place.

## A Flock of Deer by Moonlight

We moved together through the blue snow
The night was classic
And the landscape was from my childhood.

Around the ripe moon, sacred to the triple goddess,
Was a vast corona, a gem spun from cosmic dust,
A shape so perfect over so many thousands of miles
It showed a door into the stellar reaches.
This light created space to move through,
Sculpted blocks out of the quarry of darkness;
The asphodel-light whose journey has made it pure,
The owl-light of the shattering hunter and of thought,
Wheels and crowns manoeuvred in the pale day.
The light we parted, creating our own space,
Was not the golden, molten birth of things,
But the light of plans, architecture, hard edges,
Once the notes are tuned and the world is cool to touch.

Its forces stir the liquids.
Like a stake caught in the breaking sea
I part the tide and the green fury piles on me.
I'm dowsed in energy and I can't move.
The moon tugs at the masses of earth,
The fine dusts and herbs toss up and disperse,
Doors stir on their pivots. I'm shaking.
I know the light, it falls too swiftly and is
Lost; but like an image fitfully obscured
The infinite room of the night
And the endless force of my emotion
Vanish each second to recreate themselves.
The moon poured down like silver, burning
Sadness away. In the smooth black mud,
Deserted by the sea, a buried door opened.
She touched me. The memory and the
Face of tenderness

Drained my illusions.
Writing, for an instant visible,
Shining in the December moon.
Tells me what to do and what to feel.
Days, worked out in city walls,
Light, shining out of other people,
Corrupt the memory.
How can I say anything to you?
How can you share in the life I lead?

You touch me
The malevolent city crumbles into dust
The ranges of years start up like mountains
The chains of fear and loathing shiver
A metre deploys across my mind.
A thousand fancies stir, shake out, and sift away to wisps.
Animals rush across a blue space
The stars fall and their clear voices ring as one
Calm and imperative.

In that city
Where monkeys hang weeping
From the forest of inexistent trees
And a rat
Sips at the spark of sweet water;
Where I hang my face behind the door
And count from a thousand down to zero;

Where a sordid sight
Tracks across a cold eye;
In that city where my death
Drinks itself into insensibility
Sends a postcard to a former self
And wears one of two cheap suits;
Sweeps out the boarding room,
Sits in the canteen and talks small talk;
Coughs dark air out of its lungs

And sends poems to small magazines;
When I wake to see it slumped beside me
I hold it in my loneliness.

In the Urbs of interlinked immurements
Where documents track out the numbers of confinement,
The prisoner, haled in a cage before screaming judges,
Is accused of the construction of the City;
Every square yard is someone's debt
And you are born without a shelter.
Surrendered to the clashing clauses of logic
Arraigned in the due course of Justice,
In its millennia of commentated falsehoods,
Its pillars of dust and pits of cruelty,

The attainted man must only memorize
The imaginary stones of the imaginary prison.
When the Law has had its pulverous course
He says, this is my life.

But the feeling flocked like snow, it filled the sky
But went on falling, the flakes fragile as glass
Took up all the shapes here as if the earth
Was a snowflake sliding through someone else's sky
And the snowflakes were earths draped in white.
Its motion would not cease.
The feeling tries to find a way out;
But I tremble and dissolve in it.

The snowflakes melt in my hand
And I freeze in the sky as a net of stars.

The sky falls onto the barren hills
And my skin tears to let my soul out.

The sky is a sluice filled with a million holes
And a million points of light fall through my skin.

The moon makes one world visible, shakes
Another into ruin. Memory is a lie.

I wrap the blue skin of the snow around my heart
And my flesh is purged by the fires of cold.

I remember what love was
And I fall as far as the light
Eddying down on its raft of snow
Like memories poured down and melted away.

In the night of damsons and magnesium
In the night like whitecurrants pouring into my palm
The city of slag and degradations falls away,
Memory slipped from my skin and fled splashing snow.

Lit by the moon I fell in love
With a strain as if lifting a wall upon my back.

Time came back to me
The body floating in the river woke up
In the night of grapeskins and crystal nails
I washed my garments of bitterness.

I washed the dead images from my eyes
I tore down the city of unnatural shapes
Time came back to me full of your face.
My blood burst into my veins, my crushed throat opened,
The animals of memory tore my nerves and my lungs.

We came upon them sleeping, in a hole in the winds.
Their legs seemed not to swing but to leap, straight up:
The earth is slow, they are fast, the moon is fastest.
The stag turned to outface us as his herd fled
Past the fragments of the Great Forest
Across the metal hillside and towards the silken lake.
Some things are only visible by moonlight.

When the dead season is over
The Spring shoots on the trees
Must taste as clear and sharp as wine.
We move through this glimmering parkland.
Where else can we find such a free expanse?
The king of beasts sleeps hungry on a bed of snow.
Where can we lay our heads in safety?

# In My Time of Dying

*"Estote memores iterum Elysiis coventuri"*
*"Iura deorum Manium sacra sunto"*

Who provides food for the raven
When its young kick on the ground and caw for lack of meat?
Who causes the wolf to move in bands like partisans;
And the wild dog to howl in the heart of the city?
Who is greener than the forests
Though they sing crested with gurring pigeons?
Who is the history of what is taken away?
He is Death. Take my right hand.

His name is memory and eternity.
He is commander of the 6th day.
He is more numberless than breath;
He is the numberer.
Creation was torn from his flank
With his broken ribs
In a gushing of waters
A welling of black resin, and a reek of vaporised bone.
He is Death. Take my right hand.

Doomsday sits
In a sealed chamber inside the bones of his head.
Karma pours into the outstretched cups of his hands
As actions become events.
He has the lieutenancy of history
Judgement sits inside his hollow tooth.
He is the machinations. He is the assessor.
The testimony is him. He is the exactor.
Take my right hand.

The shuttles clack shifting
The threads of iron and the threads in his chest
And the garment they weave covers his back.

His bones slide like collapsing cliffs.
These fields do not rest on mould or on a secret, burning, core
But on folds of sea, the groundswell of the crawling worm.
His segments move at right-angles to his path.
His unweaned mouth emits words of command.
He is death. Take my right hand.
Who erases a star from the heavens?
As if the spattered flux in the cramped welding-bay
Driven winging through the air
Turned from red to blind
Fireflights pitting and furring the walls?
He pits the firmament
His scarf sweeps the choral-incandescent metal
It drowns it among the dark aeons;
His teller's grid sifts the years of acceded night
Into the knuckle of a dog.
He is death. Take my right hand.


Who hoses blood from the walls of the Presidium of Police?
When the Communists are brought in
And the trade union organizers
As agents of an enemy state which one day will crush the existing;
Who follows the true-blue gangs
Through the streets of Lewisham or Whitechapel
With their ringworm heads and industrial boots
Dogmeat in a jungle without scents or rewards
When under a yellow sky
Another Black is knived?
Death, take my right hand.

He is reason
The action of the mind is a sieve with no bowl underneath,
A thought repeated ten times vanishes.
It tends from Gods to theology.
The cynic yearns to be neurotic and the neurotic yearns to be psychotic.
Schopenhauer and Lucretius stand on the white shore

The waves never fall. Objects are translucent.
The sun and thirteen moons are in the sky, but sickly and pale.
The shades live on the starlight
They do not sleep or dream
But weave ropes out of sand.
Perception is the death of heroes and of perception.
Death, take my right hand.

The dead speak metrically. We listen fragmentedly.
Modernism traces a poem in sweet opium smoke,
Its limbs are worked from twisted glass and artificial darkness.
The golden years of English poetry are at one
With the ancient laws of Gaelic poetry.
The jaw of Saturn the weigher
Hedged in his Western grave
Gapes under the island and drinks us like a negative oracle.
He is time. I lift my hand and it moves
In the severed past.

I breathe solid air
A death's head graces the wax forms
Still warm, which tumble down around me.
A star of death trawls the fretted, shimmering air.
My cloak of holes, metaphor, is under its weight.
And the searcher finds me in its shaft.
A woman comes as death wrapped in glittering black
She is pale and stands in a crescent boat on a river sweeping
From emptiness to zero.
I come in a dream of furred waters, dead animals,
Teeth growing in the middle of hair.
She is death. Take me by the hand.

You so fair and full of flesh
Walk through me and the blade of your body
Cuts the level in my diaphragm.
My death glides away through a labyrinth of veins, surges.
Thinking of you, I walk from the factory at six

Pull the husk off a blade of grass
Or clean my shoes
And the action occurs simultaneously across the river.
Time is married there, where blossoms and fruits are plucked together.
The bird about to take wing from the sunlit tree
Is replaced by
The bird about to take wing from the sunlit tree.
The cloud shadow about to sail across the green hill
Merges into
The green hill about to close its gleaming eye.
Who claims to understand love
His witness be the nuptial flower
Is condemned to repeat it.


Who claims to forget love
Lesson stained into a seed of wheat
Is condemned to repeat it.
You kissed me: memory was in my arms like a wild beast.
I was free of past and future.
    You say:
                I want you to throw your arms around me
                Like a circle around the sun.
You stipple the blaze of noon.
You give birth to me as a gem, a bud, a flame, a running fox.
This ancient world still drops its young of days.

## Sympathetic

We mirror each other.
The light reverberating
In broken glass, unmatching images
Scour each others' skin.
Cloudy shards and streaks of rust
Invade the swell of your flesh.
The river of light
Throws out the nervous freight, the ash;
The joint shape rips itself up
We can't see each other any more.
The light washes around us, mocks us.

## Sickle Moon

The moon is a curved goddess sailing in a black sea of death.
She casts ingots of images, that freeze the flow and give it sight;
She drops a farrow of weeks, both replete and pining.

She quarters the earth for rivers and gleaming waters
She falls on your hair the colour of ashes
She falls on your skin the colour of milk
She strokes your bones the colour of unshed days
She rends the sky like a sickle: ascent descent
And the narrow divide.

A thousand sickles in a thousand raindrops
Needles along a telegraph wire are the seconds of time.
I clutch a doll of you
You tear me doll by doll
Caught in the seconds, I have no shape,
I die a million second-long deaths.
The moon moves casting down events and destinies
Scattering the fine divisible silver.
What else have I got but those deaths?
In each drop, your reflection is entire.

## Heavy Wind

You stand looking out towards the wood.
I move towards you.
A wind springs up.
The heavy curtain stands out stiff.
In my blood breath blows an image of you.

A gale drowns all clear sounds.
The trees call. I move towards you.
Your hair skeins the wind like strands of rain.
The leaves on the wood turn over. The wood vanishes.
The wind catches fire.

A flight of birds is tossed towards the cup of the sky.
The air is illustrated with scent, air flowers.
A seed wafts into an open blossom.
You turn towards me.

## Circulation

You tell me about your Polish pianist
To control me and lead me on at the same time.
He calls you his inspiration.
You know what I think of interpreters-
If he feels low, it's a lonely flash of insight.
In the Cafe Royal, he leaps up to play the piano,
The sound of the last century drips and fumes like a pint of ether—
Straight to the heart.
The waiters are enthralled.
The lips of the gigolos turn pink.
The old ladies crumble like gateaux in tea
And the lustre lights drip with vain lime.

You inspire him to play like a dead man.
In the concert hall
He lights fires under the dead tissue and perhaps
His audience hears him through the day.
The dead mouths speak through me, my audience is zero,
The retracting series of the echoes
Of the Saturnian cry,
Lost and die away into trees and streams.
The nation fights nets of iron, and my verse
Is broken glass.
Aristocracy has moved away, the recipients of glory and the givers of rings,
The homes of fine language and superior feelings,
The inventors of selfconsciousness.
Patronage moves away, and we pretend to love the people.
The people have their art, and our collectivism
Smashes on the cyclic turnstile of circulation.

You don't want anything anybody made up.
You want the applause, the concert dress, the receipts.
Does he slash the husks of trauma?
Does he show the worm in the sand
Its long image? and its million brothers?

Is his green the real green? You could tell.
Is the silence softer
When the music's over?

It's true the content of these words is me
And all I am is a string of words
I'm a delusion with a technical function
And a priceless commodity unable to get sold;
For you my price is zero and my value less.

For you my art is silence
And you can't see the things I say.
For you my thoughts are hallucinations, lapses;
For you unspoken thoughts are a sign of weakness:
Whoever controls the situation makes me quiet,
My voice withheld,
Corrupted by its own silence.
And you are that person.

For you, not only what I say,
But what I think, is lies.
The images moving across my face for no reason
Frighten you. You are the one I
Was speaking to all those years, although without you
Perhaps I would believe my thoughts again.
Don't you believe
I do work in words as well as in the factory?

You listen to Chopin.

## Photo Flakes Falling

We are in a courtyard where ten thousand photos
Fall in flurries to the ground. Each one
Shows us together in a different scene.
The trees are white with images,
We wade through them as we walk.
We see the space we would have lived in,
The feelings we would have figured in those spaces.

I hand-stitched each bead of light onto each frame.
My self is strung out thin, a thousand flashes
Extenuated. You don't even want one scene.
You have the camera. You wore a hole in my eye.
I stumble away from the exposure
Into the darkness where the walls deny a space.

I pick up a crumpled positive. This one
Is your hopes in me, your desire for me,
Your face close to mine.
You fritter each drop of light into dust.
Like a scholar stooped over the scruples of an incision
I scry out the strokes of my future.

We let the pictures get ruined.
Their nitrates pour down the roofs and guttering,
Their silvers ooze with blight.
I lie down in the photographs.
Their geometry corrodes my skin like urine.

The aperture narrows a maze of years and walls,
Which tilt and crack in dying planimetry;
The rim becomes a mass
To shut each space in whole obturation.
My outline is a shaky leaf of light,
A spectre flickering in mimicry.

## The Winnowing

I see you vanish in the middle of the room.
I count the years ahead and they vanish.
I think of you and the thoughts shift, they are lost.
As I touch you, we fade away.
I think of the place where you are and it has gone.
One, two
We can't move three steps.
We gasp upwards in the mouth of heaven.

The gates turn on the thole of slow bronze pins:
The flesh is slow, interpenetrated with masonry; rarely
An image falls from the burning circle
Where the animal Principles are incised, swirling
Rich as a silver Persian drinking-bowl.

The angled brows of cornices and the fire-sealed courses of brick,
The documented walls of houses
Were not staunch.
The fixed edges of thought were vague and porous,
The rigid paths of life trickled away like hot metal.
The Spring is heavy on its slender stem.,
The choice ornament fatigues by its profusion.

I run to and fro
I see us falling into the mouth of the sky
There is no staying
There is no building of day upon day
There is no movement; only the surrounding data
Disappear.
The fine blades of the winnowing air fan,
Their curved tips feel out the lift.
The feeling finds us, tries us,
And searches for a way out.
What else have I got but that feeling?

If spume rises
(Dazzling the foamflights, the radiance
With the pure core of salt
Flecks the mirror of the sun)
Some spoils fall to the black earth
Of all our adoration.

For you what I say is silence.
Let me tell you what my art is:
The secret script of veins
Of leaves burning, shuddering, clenching
In the autumn pyre. Moving in the heat,
They are not going anywhere.
For seconds a gleam in the darkness
Is articulated, a red wire ideogram:
"Opening. Death. Change of state."

For you what I say is silence.
The rain falls on window leads and gleaming asphalt
And the smoke blows through the rain.
In your eye I disappear.

# Black Pane and Decor

I go down the North Circular
Between the factory and the rented room
What's in my head is this around me,
It remembers me as I am.
The sound of cars overlays the sound of quarrels
And the sound of control data, above
The sound of wishes in my head.
The wishes fall and blow away, the voices
Slur and recede, there is no hearing them.

I reach my home & I make myself into a picture and assault the picture and rip its surfaces and open up the signs it carries and melt down the surface in a slew, a melt, a tide; and the picture empties; and I polish it down to black glass; and I'm lying on the ground as the black pane. I sprinkle it with stars for my diversion. The rain glints on my face. I'm staring at my drained face. I'm looking at a window and the window is my self and I make pictures in the window. The pictures I run when the rain falls and no-one comes to call. In a town far away a black-haired woman walks towards me.
    I wipe the image and make a garden in Khorasan, Where a minstrel in starred robe sings to a rustic court. Your last breath came from a wing: The bird outreaches your palace. The ways of sweet water and the apricot groves drop back, And the salt sea spume flecks its talon. The bird breasts the columns of air, Until he reaches the very high valley, the fell. In the snow a smithy stands, where a dark man Makes birds of bronze in burning skies, nearby An apple tree is darkened with red dust. Under the tree is a girl. In her eye is your image. The image fades The pictures are defined by my absence; here is the line of division, an iron band; a containing spar. I can't see myself. I can't reach across. You couldn't see me. The black pane is the self. I create a self in words it falls apart. I make a self in thoughts it falls apart. I create a love in thoughts it falls apart. The blackness concentrates in the eye, its images washed away by a blank precision. You'd say, the wall of that White Block where I spend my days, or the visual surface of the columnar reports, of money and time. The blackness is finely

textured; deep and even. Losing you solved a lot of problems, emptied me out. I've got spare time now. The black pane is your eye where I am nothing.
I wipe the image down. To the *Urheimat* where the bards Gwion and Wheat-of-Song
Wearing the shawls stitched with moon and stars,
The robes with jingles in the hem, debate
Over the brazier of smoking barsom leaves.
Gwion says, I know the language of gods, of men, and of animals.
   I am looking for my last composition.
      In high places
   The eye of blue ice and of the eagle
Meet without lesion, pure in the sight of Khors.
I am drawn to the mountains in the region of blue light
Where breath draws deep and strenuous and round.

Where jaws of iron bite the Captive who foresees and bleeds and loves.
I will rise through the bands
Of archaic dialects and wild forests,
The ranges of pristine rulebound metre; passing
Beyond, into the ultimate North where the crying sun
Is quenched in the seas of pure ice
And its drops harden into gold, as here
Into green; where light metallises, dropping on the strand
As dew from the rollers of dawn
Or meteors from the iron leaf of heaven.
    Breath is the pulse of knowledge,
   Running in inner and outer things;
Scaling, the courses of the body race like scouring streams,
A column reared and penning back the fall; and
   in our onrush
The parts of the world reach their greatest force.
As dimness falls away. I have no mind to come back.
As my life spills, blood ingots red on the high firn;
My last song will roll
Like the stars running nine times in their circuits
Great winds will boil from my lungs,

And stir the dust on the plain where men stoop to dig.
The eye which foresaw is replete. The darkness closes in on the pane with a steady, edgeless flicker. Quenching the points of light. Wiping each part of the cherished image. Serial logic in cadence towards zero. An ordered and causal decay. The world falls out of the picture frame, due to the carnal nature of the eye.
memory is discarded
Like something bad to eat
The eye is part of the grey listless flesh that slips beneath the tooth.
The food devours the tooth
Soaked up by the swelling
tissue of the inanimate, the Soulless Breadth
the dumb interior which has no skin, no eye
the unwriter of language and of my caressed forms
the wordless which words fail to know
Speech takes this up and is a lie
Fantasy takes this up and loses velocity
to be shed as dust on the floor. Dust glimmers in light.
The black pane is an edgeless shimmering plane. The black pane spreads to the grey rim.

    Your formal rigour slackened my shape, force bleeding out of it to perfect your ideal, who cannot fill your arms. You want it all and I am found wanting. Your need is my compulsion. You reach out and we separate. You wrecked me. The things you want would fill a house. I can't even recall your face because I see too much when I think of it. Two shapes collide in the same space. I'm the lost outline of your fantasy, I fell short. Your ideal laughs. Fends off the squalor and the anxieties. Has money and power, makes a hearty noise. Firm outlines, inexistent. You fend me off. In the comfort your feelings are clear. I am existent. Your wishes tore me in parts. I don't have feelings because I don't have power. My love drained, puffed with air and called confectionery. the room I wanted to live in has vanished, I am a ghost. I prattle to amuse you with a ghost walk. You brought me to life. In your eye I'm a pattern. Two shapes collide in the same space. You take an ideal for me and the living soul is trapped in the wood of the puppet. You walk around with a painted figment, a rig of wood. You turned me into a wraith, an airy man. My self is traced in air, inane limbs draped in spangles and tatters, a breeze spelt with the words which are my estate.

Someone wants to be rewarded for the years of unhappiness but is always punished for them. *Nehmt's mit vor Gottes Thron.* The absence he lived with half-turns into a woman and half remains absence: blindness; wrapped in a misty chill. The perfection he imagined uncoils as coldness in the face of the actual: this zero heat is that absence whose metric we have just tapped out. The sweet waters stopped in the courses, the eye ceasing to register images. Unowned, he finds himself with absolute title to a desert. I'm not the man you want me to be. The forms die.

I defy the denial of forms and the poems I write are spread around the world as Pali texts written on palm leaves, as land grants on brass in calligraphic Grantha; in white ink on cloth stiffened with a black paste of charcoal and tamarind seeds; hammered into gold, silver, copper; written on papyrus and parchment, on paper made from mulberry leaves; stamped into the republican paper of wasps' nests; on the hard parts of animals and the yielding, markable, organs of the earth itself. In red incisions bit into lamellae of meteoric iron. Fire and clay, stamped into bricks and built into a tunnel beneath the Thames. Incised in Oscan script on a meteorite deep beneath the Capitol. Chiselled in Babylonian and Old Persian into the cliff face at Behistun. In Uighur characters on a Mongol beresta, of birch bark, in a grave in Central Russia. As spells shouted for frightening off ghosts, cut on the back of a shaman's bronze mirror in the Irtysh region. By smears, by scratches, by casting. Recorded on aloe bark in the Himalayas; in India and Sumatra, on palm leaves. In China, as the grave ceremonies of the Former Kings on split and sized bamboo canes; as Daoist poems written on scrolled silk; what the marshals of the sacrifice directed struck, in Shang lettering with its stiff marching gait, on the bronze vessels in which the blood is caught. In huge ideograms made of straw and wet clay, tracing words across a marshy plain; stored with the Linen Annals in the Temple of Jupiter; as runes on the blade of swords sunk in rivers and lakes. Carved into orthogonic Roman stone in Edict Style, canonically straight registers traced by cords and ruddled with red ochre. When I speak, it's like silence. Blown into Intel 586s. Ciphered in the video RAM at B800:0000, mapping a VDU display: number 5, the bit plane specifying blackness.

The queasy aesthete scans the pattern and is disgusted by the self; the eye of pleasure slides expertly across the surfaces and shrugs aside in weariness; the portions cut from the foodstuffs in dressing are lying out in the rain, the organs stitched in complex array; discarded; tongue and eye are slack. The maze of my inner organs lies out there in the yard where the rust blooms and floresces, turning the dead back to the organic, and the functional into the ornamental; a web of pipes and switches of unknown purpose. In the tunnel beneath the railway a jelly grows purple, bold, on the water seeping from the cracked pipe that veins the concrete with a clear blood; among the Greek Nationalist graffiti and the screams against the power order and the Milesian tales of sex. The gap between me and the landscape was disgust and is the gap between my eye and my self. There's no gap any more, I am what I see. I am lonely and not beautiful enough. The lines I draw enclose no space. I'm lying dead in the yard but my suffering is too banal. This fruit of love was too bitter on the tooth that never tore it.

 The black pane, the shimmering
surface of anxiety, its even pulse, so many times a minute, across the enveloping plane, the imaginary body slurs and mutates. I cannot hold its limbs in order. Whatever I imagine is unreal. Poverty, chastity, obedience, and a hall of dead forms. You imagine me as unreal. I see a grey array. Events unroll in time made out of dead flesh. The body made out of dead time lolls in slackness. My eye is empty.

 I wipe this picture, cutting the points out of my eye, and imagine a city where the deep wells are being redug. The walls are hooped with ceramics; men are let down into the pit on ropes. The glassy water, unshimmering on its deep ground,
Revealed the head of a screaming giant.
Four miles deep, his cry made the hoops start,
Quavered the walls of the skull, dropped birds in flight,
And broke dark blood, mixed with wax, from their ears. A crew freed winched and haled up from the deep a buried and horribly decayed statue which is still living tissue, still trying to make the movement it cannot complete. the statue has corroded skin and its limbs have been twisted and mutilated; reverting to earth with limbs of bark. distressed skin, charred surface. mingled with masonry. aware for all that time it shouted into the pathless banks. phonemes torn up and blurred, words forming waves in the earth. captive flesh welded into masonry and the Pleroma, the Mindless. Its face is my own. Lips that would kiss press against the Inanimate.

I wipe this picture and the point of view sinks through billowing clouds to reveal the interior of Bronze Age Russia, spread out like a year with the seasons running from north to South. before property, before the State. In the forests the animals listen very intently to Polesin, the wolf god. In a wooden hut with carved gables a mother is singing a lullaby. You will be a leader of men, my child/You will be a singer of songs/You will be a ruler of many sheep/ Sleep, my love/No harm will come to you before you wake/ You will be the favourite of women/ The rooftile of Heaven broke, / the gifts fell from the sky/For your brother a shepherd's crook/ And for your brother a sword/ And for you a woman's glance.

I imagine an externalisation and the externalisation collapses. I imagine a form and the form dies. I imagine a metaphor and I can't identify with it. I imagine someone listening to me and my voice fades. I can't take three steps. I want to go to the high mountain, to sing as the birds on the tree. *Voglio andare sull'alte montagne.* Fantasy undid me, took you away. The surface of the room is decaying, every texture disintegrating, because my mind is disintegrating. Nothing I think is true. My eyes destroy images. The room floods with space, the cubes and tanks full of it, what space? That space where words wisp and are crushed, their cadence swept up in the flow of rotting time.

The house of paper fills with that grey flow, I excavate the self, the self is the room. the corrupt food of a starved mouth. The lies dead on the floor, the sonorous volumes coped by a marble brink. The sound wave cinct with weariness, edged with a roil of shivers where it dies. Ten thousand poets uttering the same Formulae of release, of loyalty to a code Of disanimation… As if the stasis of classical poetry is the very burden of repetitions of which depression is the impact in the earth; the crushed pounded carrier. Ossified & recurrent. *Venets netleniya*: the crown of incorruption, of bodily processes stopped in their courses, the image not fading from the eye the sip never reaching the mouth the blood catching in mid-pulse; and the anxiety is held off forever. The statue speaks, the artist is a dumb block of Past. Zero metabolism. Offered to the deathless river. *Where wert thou, envious Death, when this was done?* The statue and its voices are torn apart, severed by a territorial space, a sound barrier. The two halves of a living being.

I wipe the image from my eye and I imagine the very thing you long to see. a face in a room in a sound in a narrative. The tackle moving the eye runs pulling an empty socket, a maze of precise instructions, flicker and jitter ciphered in control data, while the living eye is cased, apart, within the stone; the living eye dressed & worked into ornament. Each hunts for the releasing pattern, the very shape I long to see. I cannot enter the room. The wish sheds my shape. The wish is the man you love and I sidle away out of hearing. The house is buried under tides of sound; the flood is the motorway noise and the pounding engines of the body which suppress what was audible. The machine of the body shudders with its metallic destructive commands. Spanned with an iron span, tensed with its thread, crushed by its stanchion. There is yet a pulse in the monotony. The wires & pales of suppression are run out. I want you. The transient precinct of speech implodes. I could not stand to hear those words. The slab presses down the pounded matter. Eye movements flicker in the suppressed image. The base of the building shifts. A vein cut at both ends wells with blood that flows into smoke and pulses with an even shimmer of spilt heat.

I tear my eye out of the image and see a class, Where an instructor is talking about nouns. Today, we study valleys. When I was underneath the valley; when I flew across the valley; when I was between the two valleys; when I swept over and down the col; when I was made of the crops of the valley; when I sowed new plants in the slopes and water-meadows; when the valley was in my eyes; when its lines and soft mosses and wild things taught my senses; when I was the valley, the valley of the river; the river flows sharp in the mountains, idle on the plain; and the river sees what I see. Tomorrow, we learn about mountains. The image is wiped-over with a black pane and the illusion fades.

Monotony presses the dark skin of imagination, juice seeps from that tense impaired skin, that lush cup of nutrients. Like a snake that strikes at glass, I spend my rarest lethal essences in vanity. Knife cuts the water; one thousand times, still the water yields and the edge is keen. The mind of hunger seeps a river of food, the mind of the exile draws whole states and countries, outlines shimmering in vague excess. I recreate you and all I see is the room itself. I identify with you and wipe myself away. The black pane is the house of egoism, its garrison. The blackness is finely divided: deep and even. The black pane is your eye where I am nothing. The words of my idea blow away.

The echoes of an evacuated language fill the air. Lies dead on the floor. What were those epics, paeans, pomps, masques? The limits of the body, overflowed by a rush of ecstacy. the personality was the wall claiming space and the society was the space which opened and invited; sound scanned that space and fell from the air in bronze resistant spans; I have neither bound nor space and the pitted casting is what I clutch in my hand, that makes you laugh at me. I eat that bronze and my face is corroded. Here is the space I live in. Here is the sound, measured by that space.

Around my body is a skin of shifting liquid lit by disturbed reflection; part swirl part shine. Blackness on the Wash, the sheets stretching out across the floodbed. on the shimmer and swell, a shape on the edge of immersion; effaced by a samite finger. Liquid shaken by sound, pictures reverberate and shatter on dissonant surface. Re-occupied by the imageless interior. Currents draft and wipe, ripple and erase. A toppling stack of faces. A lost expression. The look of love and the interior that look saw. The place of introversion, where I may not cross. The image skin. That shrinks and would be touched. untranquil half-likeness in an eye impaired by light. A slurred surface of pigment that runs and never sets. The sound wave as I speak shakes my face away. You saw nothing in my face: no blood in my skin. My expression wiped. Transmission interrupted. Clear down. A toneless whine. An even blank.

I can't find the outside and the interior of the room is inside me. Night eats up the city, its dark mouth draws the shapes away. A featureless space waiting for the figures to arrive. Light rots as it impinges on my eyes/I impinge on the soulless and there is no boundary/A shower of bloody grey matter bursts beneath my tooth/ The black pane ceases to register and unfuses into sand.

In *Geisterschritt*, tottering and fluttering. An airy man, in the empire of cloud, spinning, skittering over a hazy surface. Feathering in the sand of a pink beach. He twitters and lalls.

I have a bird to whistle, I have a bird to sing. I make patterns/ To decorate and bound and repeat/And console and fantasize/ The patterns fade in light/the black pane is my eyes. Blue fades to grey. there are no stars. there is no sun. there is no house. there is no bird. there is no sound. there is no other. there is no flesh.
Minimal patterns blurring & weathering into matter. Lines effaced.

A mouth opens in the centre of the pane. The fine ripples and swells of the blackness flow into it And it is sated.

I am a figure of fun; my passions are ridiculous.
My illusion is numb, my pain is an illusion.
The eye which sees it is artificial.
Live parts painted out, I am an image, a shaky film.

I am a figure of fun; I am a living sickness.
As a harlequin,
In a tatterdemalion trew of metaphors,
I dance a little dance of comic grief.
Besotted vengeful and derided
I hold up defiant placards in a childish scrawl,
I toss handfuls of spangles
And sell my head in painted papier-mâché.

The world in each head is a caricature,
Shaved down by brevity of sense;
In your head I became a comedian,
Gawping, and tattling some antic moonshine.
I'm a toy; a droll machine; a sickness.

## Words Versus Buildings

What have I got that you want?
Just a string of space and sound

I have a mansion with seven rooms of poetry
In the first room
I sit under a naked weak bulb
At a table with dirty plates and manuscripts
Like the table which somewhere else
My solitary reader is sitting at;
Here above
The yard with the ripped-out cistern,
The used mattresses, the woodlice, the blue PVC sacking;
Backing onto the garage's concrete apron
And noise-blasted by the North Circular.
Here I watch over
The bodies of cans and the bodies of thoughts
The death of property,
The death of flesh after labour.
The objects are the lost terrain of your body,
Their dimness is telling of my nature.
A boundary drawn all around encloses
Each day becoming me as I consume it.

In another white room
I record thousands of manweeks in
  Strict categories, watching
Work become capital.
I have no skill and my work is a clipped stack of paper.
I plan the factory two years ahead and the future
Is a ragged chart of erasures, a grid of fatigued intents.
What more is thought? expectation projects
Failure and lag towards distant goals.
Once, an arrow darted into blue air
To imagine this, which we built

For our dwelling.
Such the burrow, such the animal.

I stretch myself out like a canvas. What picture,
What voices, blowing in drugged and actless nerves,
Fill the hollow membrane of these rooms?
The mind at rest is no mind and I hear
A chorus of the dead. I know
I'm not sincere and I'm not the man I seem to be.
Objects won't answer to my words.
I can't understand the way I live,
I can't sleep for the things you said to me,
And I can't wake from this trance.
My weekend was a hard shift
And my happiness was no deeper than my picture in your eyes.

What for do I see you? If I can't sleep, I can't work.
Your accounts didn't balance
Before business started up on Monday;
We're failed tourists going on a weekend
To become someone else and finding
It was as if you weren't there.
Leisure's an empty photo, and the mechanic visceral commands
Scream like trains.

Pricked by vagrant pleasures
In the grand fumes of delusion I
Raced forward to the deletion of memory.
Cease to be what you hate, cease to be!
Tear out the bones which held you up
And stop the motion of the earth
Which bred the heaviness you feel!
Erase the face which was once unhappy!
Knowing no more I
Lost you in the first twilight.
Inside it's like a factory, and the weak are searched like wounds.
Emotion is inhuman

Feeling is as damned as perception is,
The soft surface mutilated by impinging light.
Laws impose their consequence with no breaks
Nothing is
That was not made up of a thousand finished parts
Pieces of the day. The traces will not be burnt out.
Perception, memory
I set slight store by.

Paint me on this backdrop
I live in London and you live in my home town.
This city's a disease, and in reach of the natural heart
You eat with my family, who I spent my childhood away from.
They like you better than me.
Outside, a motorway,
A river burning fragrant Babylonian oil.
To my west, the temple
Shared by Jehovah's Witnesses and Greek Orthodox;
To my east, the railway carried above the New River,
And the Elim Pentecostal Church.
In that street, a woman asked me to pray for a passing,
She said, I looked like a priest-
Black clothes and a gaze white as pentecostal flame,
Licking up thoughts and bearing them to the blank of heaven.
You see no lover's body in mine.
I insulted her and refused to pray,
But if I have no comfort to give out in my atheism,
My words are lies. Thought, as it breaks the sill of whispers,
Is spoken to someone who does not exist,
Outlining things we can't have.
He who calls my name, his name I call.
Our hands clutch at what they can't have,
Thought comes about because something is missing.
The kestrel couches on the throne of air and light,
His wingtip flick upturns the earth
The fox possesses green scented shires, and there
He burns in the dewy grass;

The deer is the dappled forest moving, and there
He plays the lover's part;
We have no place to lay our heads
Except the words I made up.

Absent, you are no more than the doll of memory
And I am the doll of that doll.
I fold my two attenuated yards across the bed
And watch the moon through a wet pane.
That girl, who was she. I believe everything you said.
The decor goes dark. My hands fall open.
The moonlight which makes phantoms seen
Drops down a silence in which the poem is heard.
Beautiful phantom, pay me with your broken silver
And lend your intermittence
To my burning strophes!
The strips of property and the bites of long debt
The rooms you did not want to share
The population and the material culture
The church, the bridge and the ragged manuscripts
Whirled around me in a gasp of song
And in their rhythm the forms fell away.

The ruins of heaven
Fall like fruit to the unmoved ground.

## Perfect Skin

Blocks dressed from my body with edged tools
Compose the walls of this town:
White and deserted
Flaked and refaced to a tranquil gleam.
Whatever is scored into these flagstones
I think it is my sentence.
The rare breezes flow across my parapet.

The snake spurts through the flaws of the earth.
Milk runs over the teeth of the reptile;
My jaw closes.
Dark and odorous like solid smoke
The blood of the lizard flows through my veins,
I think bright reptile thoughts; the pineal gland
Colours my skin, flushing it with heat and pattern,
Opening it to the laden air.

In the Orchard
The snake glutted with gold and oils
Winds around Eve's white neck, its words
Glitter and susurrate,
Flow like a rill of wine and broken glass,
Suffuse her skin with a pale fume.
Where the fruits so rich and swollen burst
The juice drips onto her shoulder.

Out on the hill
The striations of the rock pulse with red,
Its flanks rise and fall with saurian breath;
It rears in mimic battle, stains strips of territory,
Its skin breaks out in welts and combs from lust,
Rank exudations pool in crystal resin.

How long must I lie here,
Cradling my stone head in my soft arms?

The walls of the cistern have fallen in;
I can't lift these blocks. I can't reach out my hand.

Ice on the unperforated facade
Forms an eye where light moves
Till a milling of false tears flares and refreezes.

# Heavy Metal

The motorway goes past my house.
The big sound flows around each object,
Uncoiling in a thousand sonic holes.
We all play electric music, lining
Our living spaces with ghostly bars.

The music sounds like the motorway, they
Match and merge, adding
Up to silence.
I flip out in the silence like a gliding leaf.
It's not the engine noise we suppress
But other people.

I'm listening to my guts (big flesh sound,
Metals pulsing and masses pinning out the bones)
And they sound like the endless highway.
Inside, it's like a factory.
I go up the road in the morning
Haul back down the road at night.
Everything which moves is standing still.
Everything which stands still fades from view.
I'm motionless on the Long Highway
And it's passed right through me.

In the rooms
Two people talk but can't hear each other.
The hot metal closes it out
The sound the TV makes shuts it out
The sound the body makes wipes out other people
But they're not needed here.
What would you say
Except, the noise was and it's not going anywhere,
Nobody moves, nobody gets hurt.

The cars crawl by never changing
And my brain repeats the sounds of last week.
The motorway flows like memory
And I work to abolish sensation.
The metal throbs like blood in a vein
And my body pounds in rage like a motor.
The cars slide away to let in new cars
And the glass skin lets no message through.

The landscape depicts the wishes inside us,
Eight million people wanting somebody to suffer.
My nerve-ends register the flecks of the outside world
And I throw them away like glass beads.
Those worn neural tracks carry their weary freight
In a circle.
I smash up public property
Smash up refined values
Smash up my memories.

## Literacy

Carthage
Polis of sea-Bedouin
Seven hundred thousand souls
Behind the screen of Syrtis, the shifting sea-dune,
Graveyard of ships above the lost city:
The bay was once a plain.

Carthage
Laid out on axes according to the stars
Ruled by the council of the rich;
Foam-droplet of Sidon, the city of glass;
Entrepot of the Western seas, thief of the alphabet;
City of capital. City made of tablets:
Calculation, interest, accounts of debt.
Did your warehouses burn for seventeen days?

Bringer of letters to the Western savages;
Ruler of Sardinia, Libya, Spain, Malta;
Of bale-depots at Tartessus; of loans
To the native chieftains; of wharves
And mining concessions on the Tin Isles.
Did the sons of the Syrian earth, the bed of Attis,
Plough the freighted seas and hazy landfalls
To the Cassiterides?
Did Sheba furnish them her rich scents?
Was there none left in the sacked city
To scratch the scabs of remelted gold?

Reduced one last time to a commodity,
The city marches off as slaves. The State
Redeems its War Loans. Capital
Is human subjugation. In the market
Slaves jump and frolic
To show their health,
Airs upon a dexterous stick.

Near the ruins
The Berbers graze their flocks,
Using clumsy clan-signs
To mark their sheep upon the flank,
Their women on the chin.

Now the desert of sand
Reaches towards the desert of signs. In the burnt treasury
Or the house of archives, the tablets remain.
They are stylized pictures, nicks for limits;
Cadmean clay of the Recording Angel.

Aleph. The bull's head no more dipped in water-flowers
Multiplies across the plain of unfired clay.
The cow is money and its calf, yearly interest.
The images in the yeast of the brain have turned to stone.
The tallies of symbolic flow
Are the figuration of an empty space.

Beth, house. The Prince is in his palace.
God is in his temple, the high mountain
Or the heart of the serf. The slave is in his barrack.

Daleth. The door which opens once and closes once
On nothing.
The nomad's tent of years
On the plain of milk, the shepherd's course,
Before the silver cord is loosed.

Lamda. The yoke.
The captive is yoked to the mill of the world.
His nerves are the belts sheaved round the little wheels,
Straps compass his forehead.
He walks
The stones will not move.
He walks
The traces slip under his prickling skin,

They hitch to his bones and his ideas.
He walks
The blood darkens his skin.
The stones stir
With a terrifying glacial roar.
It is the anvil-bone, shaking in his ear.
He walks
The quern-rod,
The world-tree, the spine's lurching pillar, starts up.
He walks. He rests by walking.
He does not move. Earth and sky move.
Time starts. The world-mill turns. Where the null was,
Pours out a world of forms.
In the storage-pit
Are all the stars of a winter night, flour
Thick as the soil of the fields,
Enough for daily bread till August
He stops.
Everything goes quiet. The world has stopped.

Reph, man. The peasant scraping in the mud
Pauses in the heat of noon.
The serfs entered in the Temple Rolls
Know no rest. The baked mud
Has valid power upon the demarcated fields;
So many bushels per acre
Scored in my cuneiform.
We exchange symbols for corn; three fifths
Of the harvest. Such is literacy.
The dark-headed folk
Ask for talismans, scrolls
Charged with the magic Word.

Tav, the brandmark. The caress of iron.
The symbol which holds. The binder.
The technical enhancement of the skin.

Teth, theta. The sun-wheel,
The gold of wedding-rings and the red of dawn's rim,
The lifted lid of the furnace, the swooped triumphal arch.
The lord of the twelve-spoked chariot
With the coachwork of gold
With the axles of light
Races the upper plain.
A turret of steep metal
Weighs on the furrows of the earth.
The dark-headed people stoop in the fire of noon.

The villages produce corn: we produce tablets.
Sheaving stone, impropriated harvests.
The corn is waggoned in. The towns swell like archives,
Baked mud coding the tilled plain.
Assessments mar the peasant's heart like stones.

We squat for years and scrutinize the tablets,
Our gaze trapped in the interstices of the plates.
Bureaucratic class
Serfs of fat and rote memories
Oppressors of all that would deploy in passion,
We are the numbers of the lord's dreams.
We quake and turn like cheese,
Arrestors of the impulse before the threshold,
Processing the numbest of all delusions…

# Flight

The tree windflayed on the high moor
Curves in the blast.
Every limb is twisted,
Braced on the incessant loss.
It throws its arms up to its head.

Thirty years. It has not run very far.

Its inner waters are the distillation of flight,
Emaciating as a drug.
As if it were a note hung on the bell of heaven,
That has no follower and no sister-notes,
No awareness no message and no relief.
A dark cry clutching the light air's face,
The wood gives tongue.
The wind hears the prayer and the voice is wind
And the ravager of greenness is the East wind.

The tree is nailed crooked onto its own shape,
Which is purer and colder than the wind.
It is a word in a dead language,
A church whose hymns are crimes.
It is a fish in unclean water;
The eye of the water in the shadow of the night.
It is a peasant tilling rock;
A stone in scree.

The tree suckles on the rock and causes it to bear.

When the tree tore its flesh from its root,
Its mother, and fled into the total air,
It was a swarthy and a driven man.
He sang.

## Flayed Inside

Those flayed inside are obedient without question.
They forget to stop and don't consider themselves.
They notice they haven't put on the guard or the cowling,
They notice their mistakes but they can't learn.
They can't see themselves doing it right.
What do they see?
They lie, or forget to lie.

Those flayed inside can't hear their favourite words
No fantasy laces them, just words that won't wash away.
Luxury and drugs find no surface to attack.
Drink puts them to sleep but nothing moves.
Speed keeps them awake and they get angry
But nothing moves.
They talk to themselves but they don't listen.
Obsession hides a lack of interest.

In those flayed inside
No thought, flying into the inner chamber,
Brings warmth. Streams run from nothing into nothing.
Days don't add up
And the fumes of books or money shall not still
The night-stalking, chiding, appetites.

Those flayed inside march in columns to uphold
The span of alien fields, their dressage
Improves on the crop-stands of the burnt earth.
They worry about their equipment.
A mirror replaces the triumphal arch.
Twin armies march east, west. Fire is born
And the earth devours them to still no hunger, torpidly.
Null victory is declared
And the access, the fit, subsides. Whose illness?
They are not glad it is over. It is over.

# Tamur Jan

*"Tell me which way that blood-red river runs?*
*It runs due West into the setting sun."*

Animals pitch their territories here,
The fox the rat and the scavenging sparrow;
But their veins do not hold what they should
And their bones are fading within them.

Another creature breeds here
Scuttling twice by daylight,
Shifting in the factory that demanufactures him
Or laying out his wares for display—
For whoever wishes, may buy,
In the shops where the food is raked by petrol fumes.
If a tin is missing, he knows it. And this is what he knows.

Here in the twilight of forms
The tasks of man are work and death.
He does not see the orb blood-red and going down
Nor the vault lifting to admit the white scimitar
Above Bowes Road, the railway, the New River
And the Elim Pentecostal Church.
Here preaches the Reverend Tamur Jan, who has worked miracles.
"Born to Islam, I was saved by the revelation of Christ"—
Which removes clinker from the bone-joints, used coins
And demons from the airier canals of the veins.
"Sermons in Urdu, Hindi, and English",
In the tongue not used by the Mughal overlords but by
Their mixed army, ravenous with howls;
In the tongue of the Northern peasant,
From whom the divine hymns, sutras, and chronologies were cut off;
In the tongue of the dismembered world-empire
Whose servants are torn limb from limb.
*"Come close to the River and approach the Sign.*
*We will wash you clean of bills paid and bills to pay.*

*All the works of man are sin.*
*Signs and wonders before Zion pass through the eye*
*Down the seven times sealed way of power*
*And wake the worm of the heart to its duty of praise."*
Those spiritual moves I used to feel
And swore by the oath of my body to let flood
At noon at midnight and
When the exhausted smoke full of salts drowns the white
Shapes of the revealed world
Are lost.
Those kingdoms, the glance, and the desire to see
Are as dead as the roses
That were chalices where the dew burst with light.

The defeated population drifted down World's End Lane, Green
Lanes, and Powys Lane.
I split the cold rainy night
Like a skull whose eyes are hungry for pictures.

# Piccadilly Saturday Night

"Here is the incarnation of all mortal desires,
Here is their mortality.
This is the hour to be seized, gentlemen; these
Are the true limbs, thou art the man.
Here you know all other dreams are vain.

The whore, his face entirely of ceruse,
Draped in scented animal skins,
Drops of blood sparkling on his teeth and eyelashes,
Brushes nimbly past the seller of sweet peace
Dealt in twists like billets-doux or ampoules like glass tears.
Tonight's the night
Each sensation is just a pressure on a nerve
And this acre is just an extended nerve.
Each pane of sight is a facet of your holy desire,
Each face a reflux for your cupidity.
What is man but a carious film of sensations?

Ninety million visitors to London each year,
And each one demands to see one place only.
Without prejudice, these are Man's key images;
If they could carve the clouds
They'd make a three-mile harlot.
We accept all foreign exchange;
Something had to replace the factories.

Tonight's the night we sing beyond oblivion.
Sublimating the stinking masonry and its owners
You will inhale re-realized Iranian capital
Cut with brick-dust.
Istanbul is younger in vice
And the Rue de la Gaîté appears tranquil and reserved.

All around you, sir, are the rich,
Who treat their wishes as they deserve.

They grew in the Hanging Gardens, I can assure you,
To be the external conscience of your suppressed desires.
Leno assures you thus; if you won't believe,
The next jack has more courage, spitting out inhibitions.
Five minutes ago, Miss Shotsilk Liquid Crystal was here,
She is thirteen.
She draws a million dollars a day.
She turned down Morguevilliers' next film.
Her body is full of holes, calices for layered perfumes;
Her face is made of shards of glass.
She has just bought three tribes in Brazil.
She lives on squid and ambergris.


And what have you got that's fabulous,
That pulls in 1980s rent
And a sharer of your premises?
Do you think anything but money
Can buy obedience? do you think
That our conditioning can be repealed?
The way it is now, the heart is weighed against a feather
And pleasure against your liquidity.
We can help you buy your nervous system back;
I can tell you're having problems with it.
This is the true shrine, this is your heritage;
Tonight is Saint Anthony's Night..."

The bitter morning light tears down the buildings.
To my flank I see
The packs of white dogs fanning out
To run the weary down
And eat the flesh laid out in these pictures.

# L'Algérie, c'est la France
*(said by François Mitterrand, 1956)*

One does not flutter when it comes to defending the internal peace of the nation. The départements of Algeria form a part of the French Republic, the inspiration of all mankind; their hardy pioneers, rooted in the bled, extend our arable like a terrace over the sea; the indigenes, of whom so many already work under our kinder sky, enjoy French citizenship and are represented in the House of Deputies. The only possible negotiation is war. The northern part of our nation will never be separated from the southern, the ultramarine. Algeria is France, France is Algeria.

    Ulysses' keel like a quill parted the double plumes, of the vine and the oasis, of the Barbary Coast and of Marseilles, Carthage's northern entrepot. He sailed towards France and never went back. We were civilized at the same time. Invisible Tyrian purple bands our hearts. The breezes of the Phoenicians swell towards our joint adventure. Rain-bearing winds blow towards us. Valéry saw, from the littoral, clarity almost tangible hovering over the wine-bright waters. You are temperament, we are order.

    France! Sons of Charlemagne and Napoleon, the heirs of Hannibal and Augustine, their virtue encased in earth, thought for a time and shot upwards to embrace you in a newly burnished sky! Hope has debouched from the ships, a new D-Day; we land in friendship from the north, bound about with modernity; in the interior a Tuareg, whose white heat-haze robes conceal a greave of noble steel apt to deflect the surface-wreathed tusk of Toledo or Damascus, awaits French civilization in a desert hush. Stygian currents flow from steppes and prairies, twins of power and stupidity, equilibrated zeroes stalk in a twisted loop, incrementing viscous metals. Chaos counts its time. The cell itself dissolves, a fettered sickle claw. A whale rots in the mouth of a squid. The flocks of men turn to cows and the grass turns to dripped-on mud. We are not slaves and our glory is to be flaunted.

    Quirites! Christians! The law shall publish your marriage to the North Star, the guide of the perplexed. Your days shall pass in fellowship of memory and foresight. If ancient freedom stoops straight as the eagle from the solid, curved light of the morning, our fraternity is the multiplication of eagles. We are equal with you.

The idealistic young men of the OAS form mutual co-operation units, taking politics to the streets. Their destiny is as noble as history. Georges Sorel, freed from his library, is on their lips. French culture is its young people.

Algeria is French. Our capital is yours! We are the force of the age, you are ready to be dazed by acceleration. We freed Libya from the Italians, we freed you from the past. We are not the Italians, equality is our aspiration. We are not the British imperialists. We freed the Italians from Gothic chaos, and they bred a monster. We freed you and now we prosper in fraternity.

Never will the Mother of Freedom let one of her daughters fall weeping to a lower level of History. Our generosity is your token. We are not Portugal, our wings beat upwards and outwards. The dirt is absolved by the speed of the chariot. One does not compromise on police matters within the Republic's bosom.

Algeria is France.

## Passover

It was not the angel we had expected.
In the Bay of Syrtis the sandy mazes cover
A legendary city out of air; inland
A thin strip of green pasture wraps
The arids, drifts like the millennia
Of foreign rulers: Romans, Vandals, Greeks,
Arabs, Turks; then the Italians, and at last
The petrol corporations;
And now the Libyans rule themselves.
Down there in the democracy of mass will,
There by the holed, archaic tanks,
And the pillars pocked by salt,
The revelation of God
Uses Hegel's spiral for its script.
The reformer comes out of the desert, out of
The sheer strands of silex, out of the
Glass sheets of noon. There the stars have fallen,
Their geometry glints like dew on the pure man.
The desert wind blows the filth into the sea.
He tears at the paper order,
He incites the subject peoples.

So once more the Frank with his fasces
Sends out the fleet with its banner of justice,
On a turbine of lying words,
On a thick flume of spilt gasoline,
To wreck the desert and despoil the poor.
The angel flies over Benghazi.
The clap of its wings is like metal teeth grinding.
The lintel is smeared with dark blood.

# Falkenhain

*"For us there are two alternatives, and there is no third: World Dominion or ruin."* —von Bernhardi

*"The grandeur of war lies in just those features which weak-minded enlightenment regards as wicked. These men… sacrifice to duty not only their lives, they sacrifice what weighs still heavier, natural feeling, the instinct of human love, the dread of blood. The little ego with all his noble and mean impulses is swallowed up in the will of the whole body."*
—von Treitschke

*"Wenn der Herr die Gefangenen Zions erlösen wird, werden wir sein wie die Träumenden. Sind wir nicht gefangen von Angst und Schrecken und Todesfurcht? Ringsum haben wir den Tod gesehen in tausend Gestalten täglich. Und ist euch nicht jetzt, als träumtet ihr nur, dass es so etwas gibt? Und ist euch nicht, als hättet ihr bisher geträumt, und hier erst, hier an der Schwelle Gottes, finge erst das Leben an?"*
— field sermon quoted in Ludwig Renn, "Krieg"

"The fair plan allures the doomed wedges of armour
The air is a vector of iron.
The falcon lies on the white cloud
And the rabbit nurtures the falcon.
The flame sleeps in the couch of wood
And the sky woos the pyre.
Summer's golden infantry
Mass where the Winter War expired.
The smiling landscape plans a new campaign,
The fruits of Earth march across her side
And she foams a sheaf of lulling graves.
Lebensraum has become the theatre of war.
From fear of secret attack we made war on what must destroy us.
That fear left us no peace and no pride.
It is a tracker and a throttler,
It runs faster than a shell and than a hand's tremor.

We are making our children's lives here.
Gods and Aryans look down on us.
Great ages march like conscripts to the front,
Vomiting kale,
Cracks between their toes.
The thin kine of the real
Crawl back to regroup
From cover to cover.
We are making our children's lives here.
Who'd have thought the commissars would win?
They scoop up our victories
They scoop up the era and the continent.
History and humanity are theirs.

As we retreat, each step
Will destroy one yard of our beloved country.
From Volga to Don From Don to Oskol
From Oskol to Dniepr From Dniepr to Bug
From Bug to Danube from Danube to Isar.
From Isar to the moisture on our eye-apples.
A thousand villages. Abandon wounded and heavy equipment.
Abandon loyal villages.

My death is pointless, and I lie a hostage to Fortune
In his snap-brim, with his gold tooth and his leather coat.
But then, my cause is hellish.
I have no conscience. But then, Fortune is conscientious.
Conscience demands a voice, and so to the political police.
Why should I not fight? are they better than us?

No-one is of our Order and our icy fire
Who is not part of moral chaos
Who is not free of all systems, living for himself.
We are not the Kulturmenschen
Whose heritage is depression
And no estate in this world.
We are the world. Live with us in this paradise of metal.

We are the Gods in this palace of fear,
This world where human life is long since over.
We are scientific heroes: what is, is necessary.
We are the New Age;
The pincer-movement our sacred dance,
Our Thebaid the killing-zone.
Aesthetes of the luxury of metal, pilgrims of Mars
We burn the village to show where Reason ends.

In this empty wind-steppe that sometimes screams
I recall those English poets who praised what's even worse than us,
The Eastern glacis of the terminal ice
Where freedom is arraigned at the court of history.
The peasants greeted us as liberators
And we treated them as the stock of our new homesteads
Where the colonist- the cell of a new society-
Teaches the Slavs to pray, to obey, and to count up to 99.
He kills the intelligent and breeds from sound,
A new man in the heart of a new land
Developing a new civilization.
I have seen the back of many democrats.
Their speech was thinner than air
When we smashed their free and equal armies,
When we hurled the Tommies into the sea.
Now Europe is half Stalin's
And half ours.
I believe European culture is dead
And we are just the lit gases of corruption.
I am ignorant of the past. I contain the future.

Yes, in 500 years we will have cleansed the world.
We will impeach some public servants, for the schoolbooks.
Nationalism forces History and makes her bear--
The very act for which she craved.
Our historians lie no more than the others,
And we will have no critics, no purge of dreams.

These hills, these forests, these horse-steppes and sturgeon-streams,
This horizon, these skies, this black soil—may my seed grow here!
I trained here in '31. My friend Sokolov called me squeamish—
We saw how the Red Army dozed in the balsamic peace:
The peasants took the grain from the fields
And the Army took the wheat from the peasants.
One hundred per cent quota.
They fought back with flails, spades, axes, forks.
I hope I've killed him. My mortars fill grave-pits.
The last of the Divine dwells in indirect fire.
The hand of fatality,
The mouth of heaven,
Sift the numb land.
The Word
Winnows its dumb subjects.
That parabola is my parable of the life of man;
Thought reduced to prayer
And prayer to sacrifice.
The epic is the jewel of art, we were taught,
The hero is the jewel among men.
The conqueror is the prime of nations.
Violence is the surgery of strength,
Nature's ascesis. War
Elects leaders, and is the origin of States.
In the cockpit, the mating dance;
In the gallery, the virgin princess, history, hangs out favours;
The victor, wrapped in a mask of bloody animal skin,
High-smelling, shouting;
Admired at his marriage-feast.
  His dark brother, the loser,
Stands ashamed in the coarse peasant's smock.
His house is scoured in the dank earth, under the roots,
Shared with his sloven, a drudge with skin as dark as soil.
He is stopped. He is harnessed. He is silent.
One fight decided all.
The size of a man's soul depends
On the number of men personally subjugated to him.

The quantity of mastery he eats,
The reach of power he can command.
Submission is not our religion.

Yet every German but one is a slave.
Out there, the Red Army outnumbers us two to one.
Their madness is more dangerous than ours.
Once, we were their allies,
We learnt every trick from them.
From war commissar to our Führungsoffizier
From Komsomol to Hitlerjugend
From the new Moscow to the new Berlin
From the collective farm to the SS colony
From the relativity of truth
To the denial of the individual mind
From revolutionary morality to fanatical justice
From dialectic to the pure voice of the blood

Is no step at all, a step
Through an arch of nothing,
From Hell to Chaos.

Warriors blow through the passive landscape on a blood wind.
We are Cimmerians, Goths, Magyars, Cossacks… wolves.
I just don't care at all. I just don't care at all.
My rank and my alcohol. That's what I believe in.
What else is there?
I have seen the democrats break and run.
But, if twin heroes charge down the lists,
Against each other's twin hearts,
Like the right and left eye warring over the field,
Why are we losing?

Prussia was a state owned by an army,
And the army possessed by a border, a March
Where boys and cadets dream of high pine forests.
Low hills, and vast flat fields;

The landscape itself dreams of violence.
The French, the Russians, and our subject people,
Half Polish or Wendish, the internal frontier
Ploughed into the Prussian soil like a rotten crop,
Are a salient nipped in the frozen bite
Of Torgau, Krupp's, and the Academy of War:
Gelobt sei, was hart macht.
Strike and strike
Like a hawk against the bars of its cage
Is the categorical imperative.
Bred out of peril,
We are the triumph of natural heart.

In the captured town
Fresh mass graves
Awaited us in cellars and courtyards:
Prisoners, too many to be evacuated,
A card-index torn from its cabinet.
The newsreels photographed everything;
One had an open mouth, as if to sing.
What does he sing?
Obey the strong, because of cruelty. Seek it out.
What does he sing?
Guilt is unknown if endless.
Russian radio blamed us for those deaths.
Who knows? perhaps it was us.
Only the NKVD know, they hold the archives and the undealt cards.
So much for the evidence. Doesn't it go to show
You shouldn't listen to the voice inside
But to the radio?

My brother died in the Morellenschlucht last year,
The dale of the cherries, the ordnance ranges,
Where the marksmen shot for prizes in the peace,
And where the military executions take place.
Where the sun shimmered to daze the eyes
On the bright skin of the unplucked fruit,

The sniper proved his arts. He sang,
"I am a free hunter
I roam for long days through the broad chase
As free as the game I take.
Boar and deer, hare and fox,
Pigeon and falcon fall dreaming into my hand."
I proved my trajectories, leaping at the upper air,
Seeking the root and the zenith.
The shocks blew the cherries off the branches
And we picked them up in armfuls.
The victor's laurel was my brother's.
He said what he believed.
Any philosopher and any Nazi
Could have told him there's no defence for that.
Was he guilty? What does that mean?
Law is the property of the ruler,
Who deifies his instinct:
Wahr ist, was sich bewahrt.
War is the judge of history,
The test of the blood of aristocracy,
The weak are criminals against Nature.

We rode out into the world
To seek the truest of all trials;
The lots are cast upon the flat shield
And Europe is shared out by the fall.
Now we are caught in the endless Eye
Where the peasants refuse to be ruled
Where the rabbit impulses escape the aristocrat Will
And a Church of iron intercedes in favour of our death
With our lunacy.

Earth, your prospects seduced us to violence.
Land exists to be possessed,
And possession is a matter of artillery,
Its interdicts and area saturations.
The hill dominates the naked plain,

And the guns wash out the folds of the hill.
Now, you have lured us too far;
The deep flanks of the cavalry pursuit become open wounds
The tip softens in the corruption of blood
And the sorrowful hero vanishes in his conquests.
Speed, what were you to us
But isolation stretched across a void?
Where pursuit and penetration turn to loss
The silver tendon is loosed,
Discipline and rank curdle like wound-blood,
As the lips of the salient close
And the enfilade fills the horizon.
Too far ventured? what is the whole of Greater Germany
But the bulge of a salient?

The sun is a palate in the sky curved like a dog's throat
And my shells hunt like a flock of dogs in shrill tongue.
Like a draughtsman copying a Roman building
I hang a thousand arches on the yielding air.
From Neva to Niemen From Vistula to Oder
From Oder to Elbe From Elbe to Rhine
From Rhine to mothers' tears.
As we withdraw, the enemy comes with us;
I have sinned, there is no expiation.
Crime stuns my sense of guilt, and affection
Is a need I drive out. We're a disease
Which woke its own surgeon.
The Partisan, cold night's wolf, whose family we killed,
Whose wire noose closes windpipes without sound,
Will mine each yard of the miles home.
He has my father's face; he is my vindication.
But now crime is my element,
We at last are unrepressed. You'll envy us.
We are pure
Instinctive
Irrational
Barbarian.
We have become what we truly are. Animal.

Where slow clay heads crop into the cold European sky
Many have followed us, many will follow.
We drew a spark from the earth of peasants
And our rawhead signs the dull metal of their breath.
With iron we sowed the land and like the wheat of a thousand
Springs
Iron will sprout again."

# Nationality
*(March, 1979: Scotland and Wales vote to remain within the United Kingdom).*

White skulls mumble in rictus over ancient griefs,
The set strife is thawed by the warm sun of unity.
We inherit progress and not the feud;
The sky has ceased to be divided.
The orators, spooning rotting brews into our mouths,
Are dispelled by the love between peoples.
The child shall advance with an open face
Towards strangers and into the strange terrain.
Our flag means surrender: the insignia of enemies,
Enmeshed and overlaid, healed from hate.

Whatever is of worth
Was washed up on our strand-line from a distant shore,
We are close to every coast.
Timber floats from America to Caithness
And, sea-shot like gulls,
Families float from Skye to Canada.
The water washes the edges away:
Like skin it confines but soaks
What it confines with the universal
Which it impinges on: like a lake bottom,
Water strews this island with languages and spars and foodstuffs.
Flawed barriers breathe for the living.

History is a tale made up by a maniac,
Law is the calm room cradling our civility.
Our mysterious appetites fret us
Till we give them the food that's always been denied.
Open the land up, tear down
The pens. The militarized frontiers
To which our rage always tends,
Narrow but precise paths for the ravens of war,
Pools where the warrior classes breed—
Are dissolved. We move lured into the

Terrain of someone else's breath.
The ranks spill into unbounded motion.
Who would live otherwise?

I could not believe that I would come to this,
To compose with the enemies of my family;
The English courts burn the books
The English cavalry disperse the worshippers
And the land disappears from beneath the emigrants.
I have no vengeance to take,
These vindicts are such error as papistry is.
Why should the just man duplicate penalty
To demand in the second instance
What he reviles in its onset?
Or rig the fathers, dead in line of battle,
To toy muster in the strophes of epic?
Why should I remember our late wars,
When cattle-reivers died in vain for the Catholic Charles,
And illiterates fought to retain their serfs?
As for the bards chanting genealogies-
"If you should see my sister,
Tell her, whatever bones lie unmarked on these hills
Reveal the Lord's hand in the cause of Stuart."

English, lay down your crimes.
I cannot believe
That the offspring of such a nation
Own to the syllables of their own names
Whose very recital is an obloquy.
The earth grows pale with shame to bear them,
The sky pours filth upon their faces.

Once, ashen keels cooped in a tribe of mercenaries,
Native to such wood as rats to wet banks,
Loose dust pelting in the wind off the sterile foreshore,
And scum coiling off Saxon mud-flats
Who thieved upon the Narrow Seas.

The captains posted up their oars in stolen land;
The spearmen turned their wishes into laws,
Claiming title to fields and forests,
Beasts and peasants,
To the regalia and the myths taught to children.
A thousand bounds grid the open field.

English, lay down your crimes.
The tormented giant clutching the fiscalised world,
Whose blood was gold and whose flesh, the dispossessed,
The "democracy" of the failing master race,
Has died in every part, to better life.
One more colony is left, one palace of Normans.
The school texts fall apart in our hands,
Lies dispersed by a steady gaze.
Now lawful Britain has no wars to fight,
Nor slaves to guard. History has started.

# For John Riley

You were born in the accelerating silence
You were born in this newly dead language
This realm in the memory of crime,
This mirror in the gaze of no future.

In the Byzantine wastes, we lose both the living face and
The irrefragable worked object.
You knew this most of all. Learning blocks the memory.
　There are forgotten races, pilgrims from the DP camps.
The priest from Kiev and the engineer from Galicia,
The Serb from Dalmatia and the Jew from Brody
Blew like snow to this farther shore, on the edge of light.
Don't think we never did them wrong.
These are not the Hesperides.

Satem peoples, Mikola's lands
Taking the steppe from the horse and the forest from the wolf.
Slavyane, to whom the articulate word was given:
Shall the Orthodox not see in the world-tyrant
The end of the reddened age?
Shall the Chassid not work the garden of dumb stone
With the lye of piety?
There, letters are pebbles, lying on the sacred shore:
　Ace, beech, word, good, is. The object
Brought back from the dream
Is firm in the hand about to build a city.
You pressed your mouth to the chaos:
Here and there
You left stones whose order is deep and intrinsic.

In Leicester or Manchester, the black facades
Veil the fumes of worship and the holy speech.
Shatter, you piled stones!
Wisp in columns towards the vaulted sky!
You stepped ranks of frozen clay

Aligned by spirit-level and the canon of what is straight
Find your truer axis!
You grey ashlar and you purple, wedge-split slates
You yellow sandstones and you blue, fired bricks
Throw down your sway!
If man can speak, you can as easily
Cast your silentiary archives on the mobile air!


*Pravoslavniy*: just law; true words; and verified glory.
As we cross the field of gorse barefoot to the River
I don't know where the flames of candles quenched during the leaving
       ceremony
Snuffed one by one until darkness and parting
Have gone. You know.

## Deutsche Industrienorm

When I crack open that seed of thought
I call England: my home,
My name, my mechanism, my divinity; my future;
When a foreign language seems to cheat and withhold me;
When I repeat my ultimate favourite word a thousand times,
Unpeeling memories from syllables, hours from pictures, lives from faces,
I see a nation like an uncovered machine, the mill of England.
We all live in cities,
Abstract clashing waves of forces wired by money.
Our landscape is a folly of thanatic dressed brick,
Our soil, the repository of the heroic dead,
Is a dynamo of coal and a worn colosseum of metal ore.
Our skies are dreams
Where green and orange glares catch on the vaporised brass.
Our spirits are loyal flywheels tipped by the pistons of class.
Class replaces thought and morality.
Spectacle replaces instinct, art
Surrogates the sweet call of the seasons.
Alcohol turns white faces pink, like country air.
Crowds replace fields, and popularity moves our inmost veins.
Puritanism swept up the old revels into a pale fervour of justice
Resolved in a bony rosary of hard work.
Our religion is manufacture.

A frantic blade hauls us trough the viscous medium of our fate,
An exhausting, imperative, judder of transmission;
A blackletter Bible in the local tongue
Seeps through the worn leads of lightless windows
In the facades of brick factories.

Round here it's all making time, bunking off,
Expense sheets, half-sleep, card schools, tax swindles,
Scamping, painting-over, conniving, skiving,
Bad jobs, bloody minds, hangovers, resentment,
Demarcation, overmanning, light fingers,

Bad fist; quick kill, cheap profits;
Living up to being run down. God, it's so civilized.
Leisure sacrificed to work
Work sacrificed to comfort.
Bunce, rights, little easements.
They decide what wages
But you decide what pace you go.
Overweight, slow fags, no rhythm;
Tired before you start, never get tired.
The mucus in your lungs never lifts.

1880 shearing machines: they've lasted but they're
Worn out. Worn-out feelings.
Black money, no tax, take home what falls off,
No apprenticeships and hollow skills.
Holiday student, gentleman with no manners,
Knows what's wrong but he can't do a thing.
He can't do a thing. Born with a cud of words in his mouth,
Archive of slewed files, the figures won't compile.
Only the immigrants will break sweat. It smells funny.
Ten million hanging on in the Welfare Nation.
Double books, red ribbon cook, unreal city,
Accountant con, twitchy drug money,
Veins welling up, fever money, silver sensation.
Hot money spurting like eyes on the slut poster.

What's wrong?
Our expertise calculates failure.
What Americas of decay
Entice the New Elizabethans?

My generation
My heroes
What are we part of?
All we will have is coded inside us.
All we've got is here now.
England, class state, slaver, machine of aged flesh,
There was love in the narrow rooms.

In Germany the mill of work and finance is stripped down to move
Pride makes production its darling
And the working class is victorious without tyranny.
The old aristocracy is powerless and prosperous workers feel no envy.
Work is skilled, exhausting, and highly rewarded.
This is a modern state. And is my state not a part of me?

I can't cut myself off from what hurts me.
Need makes me cry out in the white midnight
Need drives our strength upon our darkness.
Need knows no I wants and I want knows no bounds.
Desire's your patrimony and want's your portion.
Your pomps and prides are the exquisite points of your hunger.
Need spawns the thought, and money
Wrings them out. Class, sex, and money
Spur the hunter of forms in the deserts of shattered concrete;
Those rank resins
Are the earth on which the fine colours are sprayed,
The pure ultimate substance of the lapped symbols.
The jaw of melancholy and the jaw of desire
Clash as the double gate of the sky,
The baying throat of heaven
Slashed by spears of sun like nerves.
Each journey starts with an appetite:
Meat is a path and artefacts are a path,
To fill the void inside me,
Which shaped my limbs to run and grasp.
Consciousness is just a by-blow.

History is the real theme of poetry-
The unfolding of mind through its instruments.
That is the declared glory
Triumph of ale and coal
Epic of skill and shifts worked.
We ourselves
The divinity of the English nation
Britain as it is.

Above, the sky, sun-theatre and cloud-sea, bright and edgeless.
   Between, in the realm of passions,
The relief of the human landscapes rushes and mills
Under control. Inexorable repetition
In which nothing is lost
And nothing given away.
The statistics of consciousness print out like tills
In millions of costed physical details.
Material apocalypse, war of attrition.

Are my seventy years of thinking a senseless snatch of oracle
Or does the turbulence of impulses trace a giant body?
Is each man a stone, sealed
In the suffocating frame of his destiny,
Or does each soul pass through all the Quarters of the City?
Are the dead brick forests of the skyline
Soil tortured, analysed earth, frozen money,
Or the shifts of our labour still living?
Is our architecture the supreme work of our morality, or is
Our thought an escape from our homes?
Is that cell-wafer of richly pitted solidity body talk?
Do we take the impression of that grid of walls
Or is that orogeny and stone archive the speech of our yearning?
Is the City upheld by men's bearing arms
Or is that graticulation the paralysis of all our flights?
Are the streets of the City the liberation of our inner space
Or is each home, workplace, run, territory,
Contested, striated, and confined,
The air-grave of a man?

   Combing the strand for wrack.
Why should they send us their raw materials?
Why should they feed us?
Why should they buy our goods? better than the rest.
For the world, we are like the Jews;
We made war for finance
And religion vanished in our love of commerce.

Honour, success, foreign policy, love, charity,
Are money for us.
We killed Socialism and turned it to wage claims.
The sheep look up to richer sheep.
Wealth is all our admiration,
Artists are loved for the money they make.
Our philosophy ends thought, leaves utility.
Our governments obey the financiers
Or are crushed by them.
On each personality
We scent the money value
As if tasting wine. Each child is taught what it's worth.

For the world, we are like the Germans: militarists.
They invaded from fear, we from avarice,
Carrying the White race to the farthest shores of its cruelty.
We were granted total power
We built up chaos and slavery.
For 50 years, we refaced our decay
With the wealth of plundered colonies.
Our ports are closed. Our protectorates are safe now.
The hunted who fled from the Slave Coast, beached with skulls,
Into the endless cosmic order of the tribal interior,
Were driven from the fully cultivated lands,
The populous farmland converted to export.
The farmers went hungry. Their sovereignty was stolen.
"We are the modern world..." We rotted inside captive markets.
Has their exploiter forsaken them? We are exhausted by crime.
Don't think about the peasants, in those lands full of raw materials,
Where the soil itself seemed a willing coolie.
We had to live off their willpower
Or else we'd have to live off ours.

For the world, we're like Babylon.
Our press has no ideals but pornography
Our streets are abattoirs of primped flesh
Istanbul envies the vices of London,

We work to make the advertisements smile at us.
Our imaginations are sterile with procurable Nymphs
Frame by frame the collective imaginary
Lays out a thin surface of paralysed skin.

For the world, we're one vast bureaucracy.
Everyone's the same: tame and well-fed.
Our minds are empty,
Our hypocritical language hides only apathy.
We turn the world to paper, look after the victims.
We have no ambitions. We watch the same images each night.
The centralized media draw in the people's visions,
Adjust the ore of passion to dance crazes and serials
And serves them up pure untouched sleep. Tomorrow, the machines.
We pay out for luxury in the coin of empty dreams.

The Welfare State is a woman, our mother.
I loved her till she brought home that recession man.
Ageing recession, ageing benefits. Slut time.
I loved that State. Time's not what I thought.
Flash London pays for canny Tyneside out of work.
The world wants none of you- and you're cored like an apple.
No thoughts. Heaven is other people.
In Germany they work for their living.
Blank looks of the Welfare Nation, class structures
Illustrate your weakened fantasies.
You have no history but shop windows,
You have no voice but our new junky music.
Kitchen boy, I wish I was a guest. I wish I was German.
We are not animals, our carnage is turned to images
And the imperatives whip-in a new language of Spectacle.
The pre-social id is corroded
And the pre-personal is Mass-man, the daylight rat.

Freedom is relayed through stone webs of algebraic form
Each gesture is steeped in years of learning.
Only envy makes us react to higher things
And our fantasies are drawn from fashion.

By the Thames, crimped aorta of an empire
Burnt and ascended to the skies,
Of which only the ruling class and the big firms survive,
In the City, money thrashes like the suppressed sexual drive
Of the dead souls being traded. Gabble and slaver
Of hucksters, repressed motion of machine-minders
Poured out as a frenzied jitter.
Sex doesn't cause neuroses, money does.
Here the secrets of all those firms
Are spread out and hacked up,
Precise knowledge in frantic brains.
They buy up your papers and wipe out your name.
On the Floor
They cry like barrow-boys in those famous tones.
The fantasy of Capital maintaining itself through changing forms,
The supreme collective myth of price;
The name of the material world, the exilic meaning.
You live the results line by line and forget them.

They are writing down the future-
Script of decaying plant and written-off skills.
Victory's the mystery, the fleeting queen, the lost name.
You have counted every derelict site, everyone unemployed,
You have listed the regrets, made files of the known.
You can cross town to find the special house.
But can you cross Time to find
Your severed face?
What is the voice that tells your errors?
The freeing from work discipline
Is the unleashing of memory,
And after memory, a glimpse of the mirror of desires—
Perfect
Self-willing, self-seeing, self-correcting.
In seconds the chance vanishes and returns.
We have our debts to gamble with,
Our frustrations to give up.

Opportunity is narrow as the blade of breath.
We can all think of happiness.
With what sure arm
In what virtual space
Do we retrieve it?
What blue knight
Through a sealed landscape
Carries what favour dipping on his lance?
Policy's a mystery, not truth;
If I can hold what's inside us,
I can't hold what's on the air between us.
My thought can't make my future
And all I hope for is outside me.
What we don't understand as one
Is lost to us.
My desire and possession
Is on the air between us.
That force is rarer than the breezes.
Law only covers the dead situations
And leaves the heights free for Government.
Truth slips off the surface of actions
The just state spins individual weakness into policy
Weds obedience to self-will
And turns conjunctures into music.
The strong state is precise as selfconsciousness
Transfigured into Control.
England, exilic Eden,
Under what sky will you flower?

## Yellow Ice, Enfield

Imagination live imagine as the yellow night canal
Has no voice beside the ordnance works.
Musaeus is an outpatient in the '70s.
After TV, no emotions.
                No memories haunt sedated sleep.
No talents and no rewards
                No humiliation is no praise
The landscape has lost its heart
         A wild hunt sleeps far beneath Enfield Chase
Radio Fun approves uplifting phonemes
           The dice of unweighted words, colour of ice
C.P. Snow approves Angela Thirkell
                Flowers cheer hospital wards
Empty stories chat to stress headaches
              Regressives weep over pointless games
Passion was a fashion
           A fantasy upheld by a class
The bureaucratic class in youth feels art
           Their bodies furled like damaged buds
They get themselves sorted out through crises
        Claimants ease the tensed bow of prayer
Production uses emptiness in therapy
        On this blind pond floats sewage of lilies
The modern skull is formed on the Nissen hut
          Our graves are vetoed one-way files
Concrete around and in my head

     Blood of concrete seeps from my open mouth
Five years going down, I hate that sound
        I can't stand the silence, I hate that sound
The senile man in the gables snuffles
        He touches the collective mind, but not I
I… am talking to myself

　　　　Gaelic is dead
　　　　Gaelic is dead

The seal of inspiration bursting the ocean foam
The green bloom of the Bronze Age of the heart
Gaelic is near dead, the hawthorn hedge full of forms
The ornaments of the families of bards cherished by the aristocracy
The ascenders of the whirling Scythian chariot
The captors of Rome
The harness of Ossian is laid in the earth, the children of
Donn
Return to him
Gaelic poetry is unprinted and unread
English is face down in the same lake.

## Rats and Monkeys

Shake, shake. It's not a bed-frame jigging.
It's not anyone rattling a door-handle.
It's not woodwork. It's not a stuck drawer.
It's 3 am and I reckon it's a rat.
It nags the wood like a lover.

The day is dead, an image lost on faded walls.
Gnaw on, old rat! whittle, tunnel, chafe, devour!
Timber, fret, tap paths, shovel with your teeth!
Your eye is brighter than a polished grain of wheat,
Your fang is keener than the edge of regret.
Your wit is tindery as fire-flint.
Your blood is the crack of acrid wine.
Your hunger powders houses. Your jaw shivers beams like lightning.
Your eye knows the dark as veins know the guts
Of coal-dark nourishment.
Daylight rats, tree rats, are sharper than you, little man.

There is a shelter, wound within the sheltering space.
Cover over our city, you see a bankful of tunnels;
We burrow blindly in the meadows of thought.
I chase a labyrinth with my teeth: speech.

Your cloister, lagged with ego-stink as if with mirrors,
Lank Lebensraum,
Rifles the throat of darkness in dumbness.

Night. Reason steals forth from its bed to roam the sodium tunnels.
Feelings crave to raid the seed, and nose in the limelight.
A slick fur lustre on a glisten of liquid tarmac...
A deft ripple of darkness
Like a spark along a black limousine panel,
Like a sable wrap and a clip of raindrops.
Night Caspar journeys to the rising sun
Star-swept.

A new-moon crab scuttles in the silt of the Pool.
Filling is trickling from the houseframe.
The skin on my face is turning grey.
London dawn comes up soft and grey as underfur.

## Machina Carnis

You device of flesh I walk around in
Tank of blood and piano of bent ivory,
Transmitter of blind forces, shear of sound,
Little state, serf and prison of the soul,
Arena of sex-clashes, image of the wolf our brother,
Validator of animal language, emaciator of the abstract,
Doorless cell, soft vehicle, white treason,
Male wife, mother of the imperfect hours

Who'll kiss me when you're gone?

# Visitors to Art Galleries Considered as one of the Fine Arts

Faces: clove-maces sopping with wafting images,
Imperious and instructive.
Suits are ironic classicism,
Making invisible by conventionality,
Disappearing like Sunday's texts of misunderstood poetry.
They can hide anything.

The strollers look at each other.
Their ornamentation covers all schools.
Flowers bridle in envy and light is impressed
At this technique of allure, of transmission.

At the Sargent show, all the punters were sumptuous
And wooden.

At the Royal Academy, the chick
Strapped into sheer, skintight, full length, plastic Leopardskin
Recalls Swinburne, asked to withdraw his poem.
"This is not lascivious, but a faithful record
Of two leopards mating on hot sand."
Not Stubbs but the Trash Aesthetic.

Teenage children of academics
Are severed nerves on glossy paper.
Lean artists are heroes drawn by Egon Schiele.
Punks are figurative razors dressed by agents of tyranny.
Fifty-year-old aesthetes have faces made rich as port
By sensual looking. Their pasts are tears of strong wine.

I once saw fifty German six-year-olds inside a gallery
All painting like Emil Nolde.
In the next room, *Freude mit Farben*.

In a family, bright surfaces are morality.
Sight lays melancholy waste.
Faces glow with it, deeper and softer than thought.
Full capillaries make the skin, quick silver nitrate,
Take in more light.
Integrated configurations sop up the traces
Where sorrow had been.
Happy hours are slung for contemplation
On the easel of icons: real Mother, real Child.

All art tends to something beyond art, beyond forms:
The transhistoric Will, self-willing, self-maintaining-
Or these real Houris of the decorative sublime?
Dear female art students! Exhibiting in your visual rhythm
   Canonical sway
Of organic
Delucidations.
Ethnic, classic, modern: wild forms with realistic contents.
   We have constructed Pyramids for the mortality of life-
Rash couture for the fleetingness of hours.
Babble signatures score clothes-like pigmented caves.

Poets don't hire models, it's not done.
   In a life-class, we could sketch superb mentalities.
No naked temperament reclines for me,
Warm and pillowed, lovely, full of lights.

Our etudes
Are the vinegary, paper tripes
Of shrewish and blowsy academicals.
Titian, lustrous bronze coifs outmatch the quiff of Williams.
Does Connolly slake our Siddall-longing?
I wish they'd close art-schools, I'm so jealous.

Bauhaus citizens develop without waste. Their eyes scan neatly.
Hope is logic. Forms are stills of the river of health.
What is a body? a machine for living in,

Factory and garden. The hand is a tool.
Mind and world are coefficients of beauty.

# Fen Landscape

Green mould grows high up the props of disused wharves,
Where the shady bilges lap above the mud.
The prow of rats slips from their cavern at the waterline,
Forever crumbling. Under the ripples, the clay is smooth as water.

In summer, we could draw down sleek green reaches
As if we slipped along a tilted bottle.
This is no time for such exertion,
The strength of the season is fulfilled in reverie.
It is autumn, the river is warm and low,
But we think only of the past and of our own fallow.
On drier land, the trees grow red or are filleted
Like textile stencils.

This fen cuts across the farmland as weeds cut, tangle the water,
Seeps lying across the tilth like smoke.
Vast stacks of wetland reeds, cut, dry on a plot.
Dredge scoopfuls lie upturned along raised banks.
Here everything is damp and neglected;
Here is the midden of all hopes— in torpor.
For miles the land is untilled.
The white reeds spear up like Chinese writing.

How many years have we lived this boring rustic novel
Called public school? Our friendship deepens
As I revel in your legendary sloth.
In harmony
We ascend towards the source of pointlessness.

Art is a river whose cunning
Is not to flow towards the salt sea.
Where the brain sprawls like miles of mudflats,
Where thought is like a cattle-watering place, trampled
Blurred and mingled brink
Where hoof-marks seep full.

New forms spawn from unwariness as old ones collapse.
Here nothing is useful, and no-one is watching us.
The river slobbers in its coils of marsh and floodlands,
Dawdling in idiotic furbelows of wind.
Willows broken bridge the slow dikes.
Duck fly up off water to part the drifting dusk.
The red sun, mist teared, lacquered on the sky, lights
Our way home across these water margins.

## Interview with the Spirit of the Age

I am the 20th Century, I am the stuff they put in phials;
I am the death of Providence, I am all masks and tunnels.
I am the latest century, and I've got to sell.

I am Fascist, Communist, mercenary, hysteric—
The insane velocity in the bone—
The hovel of Neolithic style, formed on the skull;
The glass skyscraper's pure square mile of clouds.

I am the Twentieth, the one with automation;
The intersect of camera and horizontal lathe.
I am a dream designed, written, lit, and photographed by Sternberg;
I am the films of the agitprop train.
I am the best welder, eating overtime like meat,
He looks after his mates with his example.
He is illuminated with blue flame;
In the power of metal he rejoices.
His dark passion is stellar precision.
I am the rich man's son, soft as milk. I am his daughter.
I wrote the Secret Book of Time
Someone in Memphis set it to rhyme.

I am the Ultimate, I am what's left over from the real.
I am the broken village in the trench: shards and epic fragments.
I am the soil horizon in the brain:
The steles of water and the moist red earth.
I am the general known as El Dorado and the men whose hearts are cut out.
I am the air inside the Pyramid; the hare buried under the first stone of
    the City;
The submerged gate;the furnace under the sealed iron room.
I am the ceramic lions outside the village soviet;
I am a haircut in Greek Street.
I am the connoisseur of mascara, amphetamine, daisies;
Of rhythm and blues, lightning sent down wires;
And of the musicians in green costumes at the thé-dansant
Who are known as the Penguin Café Orchestra.

I am the Turning of Time, I can do you
Some two-headed dogs; I am COMSAT and meteors.
I am dual-millennial; I am a total pin-up.
I paint my face in the glass of the windows
Of the train passing mine.
I am technical liaison
For Krupps and Schneider-Creusot.
I arranged this:
Giap beats the Americans with captured weapons,
Von Manstein retakes Kharkov from the East,
Thatcher sacks the working class as inadequate,
The Red Army massacres strikers in Novocherkassk, May 1962.
Choose your own parallels. Knit your own causal nexi.
I am spectacle, the flow of the posters and the ads.
I am Radio Moscow, the other version of the day
I am the illusory fugues, the dictation of the neurosis
I am the unreeling digits of the control systems
In the huge and unmanned factory.

I am the one after 19, the guy
From the Motor Tractor Station.
My seventh sage is rumoured to be an idiot.
I am the shanty towns, 80% of Ankara.
I speak English with an English accent,
Welsh with no accent.
I am philology and dialectic but I don't believe in semiotics.
I am the deities who got unemployed.
I am Kurds, Ossetes, Lolo, Uighur, Sorbs;
I am the pagans in Kafiristan.
I am the manuscripts of the genealogies of the MacDonalds of Skye.
I am Schiele, Fallada, Nazim, Matta, Juhász, Fahlström, Miles;
I am the Final Program and the cuneiform cylinders.
I rule the Empire of Albany;
I am the propaganda class and the point where the image cracks.
I am the scream of rock and roll in its madness;
I am Time's decadent son.

## Almond Wind

A wind blew in the region of the Black Sea.
It was like the outcry of a bird.
It carried enough almond blossom
To hide the surface of a lake.
It blew
A note so pure it drank the enthralled air
And drifted on the European shore.
Where it ruffled
A face formed on the water.

The rain-bearing wind cast down a lake.
The lake has a triple form:
The choppy lake turned to a fish's cold and broken skin;
The lake given by the night an endless starry depth;
The lake firm and bright as glass
Which frees the eye and accedes to the total blue.
As in the stressed languages the steps of ictus—
Pinions, spirit hammer, quivers along the cord of air—
Ascend from height to height of lifting breath
In the tiers of stress, so
The superlative draws the mind;
As a slope draws water across the broken horizons of earth,
Through the pitches of matter.
The lake forms the image of an almond tree.

A word was spoken
In that stellar black;
A rhythm crossed the inner span of darkness.
Matter shook itself like dust on a cymbal,
Mountains froze along the globe's chords,
And a green wind raised trees from clay and light.
Then, rocks and trees moved at man's command,
And all sang to meet the rising sun.

When the Thracians tore him limb from limb
The sun died with the eye of Orpheus,
Space turned to division as his motion ceases,
The sap of the flowers perished with his fluids
And measure was parted by his dismembered language.
A generation of spectres caught up his phrase.
The poisonous yew ate up the white and fluttering birch,
And the birch sleeps frozen in the cask of yew.
Drilled masses shook the earth, marching to song,
The ash-shafts struck roots and estates in the slatted sky:
Spear-leaves, a forest of hammered sun, shimmered.
Scythians paused on the mountain hinge between sea and sea,
Cast wooden lots upon a painted drum,
And moved out onto the plain to found States.

Now, snow takes up the tongues of rivers, pierces the fruit's flesh:
And the snow takes up the buried shapes like Reason.
Thralls work the seigneurial furrows,
And a warrior caste reaps and winnows peoples.
When he unleashed the screams we still hear
The true sound of trees and waters died
And the sun was darkened by corrupted sight.
Madness slurslurs the rhythm of words to bestiality,
And the work-gang's drum beats without grace or tremor.
The mountain man stands in the middle of Saint Petersburg,
And the sycophant rhymes slaughterhouse with altar.

Where the wind ruffles the pool
A face forms in the water. I mimic it,
Worship it, disperse it, ask it questions.
How should I arrange my days? my thoughts?
Thoughts die as they flow, to leave,
Each one, a part of the measure; the safety of the plant
Is in the rhythm: how seeds pulse to recur and seed,
What men cut into glass or write on linen;
Or what strophes the wind recites.
Because what's said can never be silenced

We part from each word to replete the measure.
Oh, voice inside,
The stream bearing images between light and the dark fastness,
Which scales, shoots, sprays; is steeped and tinged and
Driven by great swept-axis blades;
You are the little breath, all
That father and mother bequeath us.
What days come to us
When that voice is once untuned?
Their air carries us to a far land.
Unskimmed by angels, we still hear
It beating around our heads. By lakes at sunrise;
As agonists in love; in
Discussions by night;
We glimpse the true and sheafing Spring, the green wind.

A pure wind wafts the white flurries;
Its scansion is higher than the rigorous stave.
Snow falls on your bare head as you turn away,
An old Jew thinly dressed among the work-gang.
A wind blew over the shores of the Black Sea.

# For an artist having died in his dreams

I
Awake in the landscape of frozen crystal,
White and markless flooding
Towards the gleaming sea edge.
A nap of blue light threads the ice palaces,
The visionary architectures, borne on a breath,
Resistant to all but screams.
Air hurts the nostrils.
We throw warmth on the air and it returns
Purged. Blood retreats from the outer veins.
Snow falls on the bleak and empty sea.
How did we come here?
What path leads from this state?
Should we gather bands
And denounce the errors of the States?
Should we dig beneath the snow?

You see
As we become colder we become
Closer.


II
Where the city borne by water
Glints on the crest of each ripple
There the self lies entwined with its own perfection.
Is this my image staring from this mirror?
The rich bell of the ripe blossom
In the Palladian gardens of the mainland
Hides perhaps its half-formed rival.
That is a bitter sight.
The sealed flawless shimmer of the sky shames us,
The intact glacis of the glass pinnacles searches us
To the last nerve.
The thin arm would like to be stronger,

The strong arm, laughing, controls the thin.
The image works the lilywhite boys like wax.

Between revolution and self-abandon
Without ambition or secure possession
Between insight and submission
To the Other, the superior image;
In the sacred space,
The pitched field marked out with peeled hazel wands,
There we struggle.
If he is a leader,
If he is a hero, artist, lover,
If he is my true self
There we fight.
The cruel Watcher is in the landscape and in us,
Making my shape weak and vague.
You made me
Clearer.


III
The crowd crawl with their faces pressed to the great square
And the legion array in stars and colonnades.
Insignia bloom upon the picked physiques.
The guide of fife and drum in walking sleep,
The thousand mirror-blank marching feet,
Hallucinate the gaze. Severed
Dogs' heads dangle at their saddlebows.
The chaussées are laid out as firing-lanes, glints
Of an ultimate beholder.
And which wish is mine, I cannot tell;
And which boots are mine, I cannot see.
The neoclassical giant façades continue our weakness.
The new order extends private hysteria.
The ranks of maidens sing hymns to the State.

Should we heave the burden of policy upon our backs?
Here in this sitting-room the pictures
Show dragons and clouds in swirls of fume,
There is no window, I cannot
Bear you to leave. Should we try
To reach the world?
You were a compassionate man.
You lost control.


IV Colony
In the rooms where thought smears the walls
In the streets with the huge posters and gutted factories
In the waste ground of the City where lovers walk
Words fall to the ground as ash.
This is the city of the dead. Here no thought holds up.
In the mazes and details of the necropolis
In the ruled spaces of the banks and authorities
How many years have been lost?

Snow blows on your bare head as you turn away.
Your labour brought me
Closer.


V  Venice
Doze on the islands splashed around the lagoon,
The holms stippled with purple flowers.
At low tide, there are miles of mudflats;
Children like artists flop in the solid unconscious
(Nearly solid).
From here Empire rained on the Peloponnese and the Ionian Islands
But no more.
Turkish banners hang inside the Old Consistory,
That swept like clouds above a bloody sea;
Down the Dalmatian coast, the Lion of Saint Mark
Sleeps beside the bureaucratic Austrian baroque,

A nursery of painted bricks.
Once fortresses withstood the Caliph's siege,
The pack of iron throats in battery. Kings,
Old gewgaws, drank in exile here.
The sweet wines of Cyprus, solar and currant-rich,
Came here by casksful. Albanians
In white floppy smocks and pompom shoes
Brought milk from the green shore.
Gilded weaves from Ormuzd were piled on the wharf.
The city is like one reflected on waves and no more solid.
The armies in the pictures have turned to paint,
The paint from capital to people's joy.
The woven iron of domination has turned to mud,
Light is almost freed.
You brought me closer.

## *In memoriam* Pablo Neruda

The armature of your lathelike mind is
A nitrate mine: Iquique,
Where you read your poems to the masses mounted
On consciousness, no more on work: they struck,
And each miner heard, in your hymns to the real,
The warring giants he was part of.
Between null and mass the path of air
Between air and stone the path of green
Between green and lower air a new layer: man,
Stone turned to unstill flame,
And your language the magma of his irruption.

You have eaten the five pomegranate seeds
Which bind you not to Hell but Earth.
Your oath splits you like a seed;
It is Spring, the conception of the real and of names...
Like a red and black wasp
With the visor of a divine horseman
Your greed bores through steel.
You swallow: nitrates, oxides, flames, flamebridges,
Piers, shafts, ores, moulds, structures.
You are ravenous for atoms
You slalom between cell walls
You accelerate from an idea to an apple-pip
And strike off a bronze tablet from the air-lanes,
With Aztec, common, heads in bas-relief,
Carrying the cores of this world not on their shoulders
But inside.

In the streets barred by demarcations and old prejudices
The man whose head by day is a lightbulb
With a filament of two inch-worms, wrestling tired,
With his features pressed into a smile
Which he unscrews and carries through dirty tunnels
Full of smiles stamped on cellulose

And bodies abandoned in some other place-
Those bodies, employed but not activated,
Whose happiness is turned over to posters-
Does not understand what he does or fails to do.
At night he houses in that jack
A skull made of black sugar
A confectionery to console his wife.
"What was the day John?" "Just hanging around."

Venus, through you
Are unleashed the hidden forms.
I know in secret
The pale and shattered statements which eat up all our forces,
The moulds of the negative forms,
Are not delicacy but lack of love.
For you, Neruda, lifebearing wind,
Venus is a young peasant, guajira.
She is strong through working, her appetite
Knows the earth, clod by clod, and would transform it.
She is not sated by the inhabited lie,
She overflows it.
Her sisters sing as they work: your songs, and worksongs.
They are the reapers of man's treachery, the tenders of another harvest.
Their beauty from the youth of Nature makes us conscious, militants;
They cast our hearts onto the high mountains
Where aspiration draws on a precipice of breath.

You move through a tide of demiurgic poetry.
The total description of matter totally transformed with numen
The destroyer of all names and the renamer in a ride from Ocean to Ocean.
The smallest of the infinitely small lamina of physicality shrieks,
In the mass of what is known and dead there is a fundamental motion.
The clear statable matrix of stresses and motions sings.
Nature is a sexual sheafing, nuptials of galaxies and sycamore winds,
Genesis of granite dikes and stone temples.
All particles are charged, kicking, directed,
Dialectically crossing,

Laying down traces, motion dying into scrolls,
Mortally ceasing to be what they are,
Seeing. And we are their life.

You tell me in secret where I'm going.
That only shared thought is meaning,
That true thought can only come in action.
Language through you tells me
Those, who can concord their forces
To cast complex shapes in steel or create a progressive movement;
Who from shards and fibres invent a language—
Society in man and force-map of reality—
Who can raise up all buildings and earthworks,
Like caryatids of thought in the unaltered temple of the sky;
Those can bring a new civilisation to birth.
They can thread the unfolded cybernetics of State policy
Through the patterned turbines of the productive classes; bonded and
       laned,
The wires of thought and the fires of faith.
The forces that torment us have their true earths;
They are just the shared members of the collective life.

After the murder, financed by America, of the people's government,
Came the murder of the greatest poet since Shakespeare.
Although livings were thin for them, the Empire's sealanes caving in,
The Seamen's Union blacked Chilean cargoes.
A single act of idealism
Foretells a better future;
A single sign of consciousness
Effaces my old despair.
The English intellectuals
To mark the death of the instress of the unborn century
Did
Nothing
We regret
Nothing
We remember

Nothing
We desire
Nothing
We are
Nothing

## On First Publication

Three years' work and it's worth nothing.
Less than that nothing worth
The dole of £13 each Tuesday from other hands.
You pay for the printing, you work on the setting.
You put it out and no-one buys it.
Amateur! The pros tell how it feels to be rich
In paperbacks as bright as sweet packets.

Who'd have thought I cared so much for money?
My years fold in pleat on pleat of yellow treason.

I'm exhausted by warring shadows.
More calm? more force? unclear, I start to shake.

I draw benefit, one of the leisured class.
I don't have to work. There is none.
I think all the time. I try to remember
The Welsh poetic vocabulary.

A principle of silence has ordered our habits.
How long? how long?

I'm almost blind with total light, with
Dew, half drunk by the sun, half weighed down by night.
I love my art; cruel sister, remote princess.

A strong man needs strong enemies:
Poverty, madness, disdain, compromise, silence.

Years of thought. At last I crawl across the floor
To put my hand in the boss's pockets.

## The Academy

The academy: rats where no corn is.
Monks fast. Famine of idealists.
Subsidies from the poor to the idle.
Aristocracy without manners.
Metrical thought reduced to essays
Knowledge rotted for lack of love.
Doubt wrapped in the scorpion of doubt.
Life lost in love of knowledge.
Subjection of poetry to the State.
Reduction of the State to individual weakness.
Here, as drinks are cured by overdose
The middle class is cured of art.

# Trotsky from Petrograd

The armoured train wails into the white night.
Clack, clack. The church of iron builds a bridge of souls
And moves in strict rhythm across to the no-self. Clack-clack.
The idol of youth, the Jesus of science,
The maximalist
Walks like an incarnated thought.
Europe hangs from his belt in dried blood.

Death to the Whites.
The cavalry reach the ships in a last caracole of aristocracy
To legendary exile. The infantry stay, unburied zombies.
From untutored proletarians to modern slaves.

Death to the democrats.
Death to the Social revolutionaries.
Death to the Mensheviks, negative dialectic.
Death to the kulaks.

The artillerised theorist visits the little villages
He knocks at the door of the humble izba.
He takes the strong son and the tender daughter
He replaces them with a poster. What of it
If his shoulders were stooped and her smiles mattered to no man?
This peasant woman is on the Collective's committee.
Look at this girl standing in her cultural context,
This kerchief stands for her maidenhead,
This textile bears symbols of the seasons,
The pattern of this jerkin means hands, plaited
Each to each. Where is the village?
Where is the land? he has taken the field of wheat
And buried a book.

Death to the Ukrainians. They spoke a bad Russian.
They fought the commissioners with forks and axes
When all the harvest was taken away.

They volunteered for Hitler. Historians don't learn Ukrainian.
They read the Communist sources. Ukrainians learn Russian.

Death to the Volga Germans.
Death to the Tatars, princes in disarray;
Russia was once theirs; they disdained to plough,
Their possession was motion, termed by night
Or the midday heat; their eyes sift the wind
And the air is their ocean.
They rode under a bloodied sky like the endless dream of the earth.
Aryans west, Cimmerians south.
Goths east, Scyths westward. Avars west, Huns west, Magyars west.
Varangians south by the river route.
Tatars west and north.
Napoleon east, Hitler east and back.
Muscovites make all directions led back to their shrine: no self.
Death for the Trotskyists.
Death for the Stalinists: Bukharin, Kamenev, Zinoviev.
Death for Trotsky.

# Office Boy

In the half-mile corridor behind the half-mile of blank façade
I pass the office-boy delivering mail.
He is fifty years old.
When he was fifteen, he was an office-boy.

When he was five years old, he was an office boy.
He was never Churchill or Alan Ladd.
The fantasy died in his throat.
This is why his mouth hangs open.
What does he need imagination for?
When he was five years old, he was an office boy.
It annoys me that he walks so slowly, not him.
You can't help these people.
He makes you cling to your talent like a purse.
You have to be attractive to attract thoughts.
The bright kids rise by their rightness
The peasants resemble the worms and stones.
He means death and failure.
He is a squat god nudging symbols irresistibly into presence.
What jubilee, what melting of the stones.
Could make him wanted?
The food loses life as it goes inside him.
He is no go as a sausage skin. He can't melt the fat.

After the revolution, he is an office boy.
His son is an office boy. The factory turns out the same goods, thoughts.
Staff and installations
Sky streams and soil
Radio beat and nervous routines
Spleen and liver and stomach, wiring and canalization of fluids
Housing and capital
Scented sweat and sour kisses, are all the same.
The million stitches of the day, knit in liquid,
Blood lymph and bile, are all the same, you have to
Pick up every stitch.

What lifted up the snowy mountain
And what melts the snows
Drives man towards beauty.
Who withholds the sun from midday?
What order keeps the real forms shut inside their dead replicas
When what we have to lose drives us on?
Is not beauty a fellow-man contented?
It seems to me, he'd walk faster.

# Oreads

Why have you come with coral feet?
Why have you come with coral feet?
Why have you come with ankles as fine as shells?
Why have you come with ankles as fine as shells?
Why have you come with steps so high?
Why have you come with steps so high?
Why have you come with thighs so long?
Why have you come with thighs so long?
Why have you come with hips so round?
Why have you come with hips so round?
Why have you come with waists so supple?
Why have you come with waists so supple?
Why have you come with stomachs so smooth?
Why have you come with stomachs so smooth.?
Why have you come with breasts so full?
Why have you come with breasts so full?
Why have you come with bodies so white?
Why have you come with bodies so white?
Why does your dance stamp with such a fearful beat,
To shatter my ideas and make my hands shake?
Why have you come with eyes so bright and full of fire?
Why have you come with hair so glossy and electric?
Why have you come with cheeks as pink as dawn?
How can your voice reach such a pitch without breaking,

Why do the trees shake in the wake of your theme?
Why have you come with brows like marble sills?
Why have you come on a midnight wind
When the moon pours down like broken silver
From the forge of nativity and longing, the spring of darkness...
Why have you come with aureate rhetoric
And measures just as constellations;
Vessels of passions, mirrors where fires are shown, springy wands,
Unsealing fountains to flood the dry ways of song?

"We are called Lorelei, Inspiration, Sighs…
When our looks are withheld, you are in eclipse;
When our eyes are wide, you foam with the revealed world.
When our eyes are harsh, your eyes are deprived of colours.
When any crown is on your head,
We are your royal part.
We are loneliness, imagination, redress.
Our forms are the borders of exile.
We are the theatre of your life, we are the court.
The soft unspoken lyric is our keepsake and we are the air,
The silent song
Of your tongue finally severed from your mother.
We are the repository of the call, the chamber-grave
Underground, in the domain of Hertha where the saps of procreation
Mingle with dead souls, in the lee of world-winds.
We come for you."

The landscape seems made from a woman, smiling or stern.
The pools and stream seem to be the haunt of nymphs,
Barely ruffling the skin of the smooth flow.
The arbours in the pine-forest are made for trysts.
The snow waits to highlight white-blonde hair.
Birds soar in the blue stole of the sky like gasps of yearning.
The narrow caves in the red rock where the living water trickles
Are openings in skin, but smell of moist earth.
The cyan-blue light seen above the polls is like a divine glance.
In the tangles of the old forest Frau Perchta is savage.
Her shaggy pelt and livid skin change, for who kisses her,
Into a queen of dazzling beauty. She is the mercy of earth,
And Her love of man. She is nothing.

"We came to pass sentence
After inciting you to crime. These shapes
You see will last for ten years, a second
World of illusion and a building of lies
Where no ideas and no desires are possible.
These fits which shake you

Are not the wake of a wind or of beating wings
Of some shape passing above you, or of you rushing past the world;
But a quiver of the nerves, twitching
For a weight you're too frail to pick up;
Then gabbling in a rant of blurred lips.

Your name is: pining; unrequited; unwished; mad.
You invoke redress but we came to condemn you.
We are not the Muses,
Bearers of the measures that would fill your mouth
Then, when the air carries a rhythm weighted by a stream of presence
That causes the mind to be whole;
We are not the Graces
Unseen, whose laughter is heard close by,
Seen, they make your breath catch in your throat,
When, adorned flushed and enthralled,
They press in a flock around Venus,
Unquiet and longing,
Unstill and sure in every motion,
Flickering in slow light strophes
Of the musicians;

Your error, metrist; your guilt.
We are the Years
Of neglect and dark and silence.
We came to wipe out this solitude and lay it waste,
And deface its seared lines and
Pave the desert with stones.
You will not hear the beloved voice say the tender words.
You will dream them and wake to horror.
Depression is a city,
Our divisions are being reared around you.

We came to steal the meaning of your words
And take away the living ears you wished
To pour a message and an aura into, the eyes
You wished would make your figure human.

You were cut off by fantasy and now flee into illusion.
After longing
Follows blankness.
After pride and disgust
Willingness
After great projects
A working routine again.

Your name shall be: demon-ridden. Prince of the devastation. Bard of
    the slavering mouth.
Archivist of the erroneous clausicules. Expert of the inane. Drinker of
    the cisterns of dust.
Mouse in the wreckage of your own brain.
You can't read your own words without seeing red,
Your skin crawling, your breath catching and wheezing.
This is madness. After us, you will long to remember
A time when you saw what is not.
After you break your own feelings to avoid dying
You will cease to see anybody's feelings.
Design
A world of zero signs, of wires, of paper.
Live there."

## In Charnwood

Three kinds of smooth: floods of the Soar, silver sheets of miles,
Black cleaves of rock, chafed and faced by forceful rain;
Slick clay, wet and split by a fork, or smooth inside itself.

Three kinds of red:
Red of hawthorn hedge, like a haze on the meshed twigs;
Red of the outcrop of rock at Mountsorrel;
Red light in the afternoon on walls, faces, clouds.

Three names of the province;
Coritani, worshippers of the Goddess Trent;
Raisers of the earthworks at Caer Lyr.
Mercia, the March: the military frontier. Landless mercenaries
Gnawed the Combroges to the bone of garrisoned Snowdonia.
Charnwood: burnt forest. Before America, this Great Wood
Or Hercynian darkness of wolves and mistletoe
Fed the seaward colonists.
Ash-keels tilled the North Sea, swan's way;
Fire drowned the stands of oak and beech.
Ash as rich as coin and fine as silk
Mulched the won fields.
In February, the burning;
In August, the reaping.

Three kinds of yellow:
Yellow of corn in July, Iraqi reed turned to fruit;
Yellow of hair, blond Danelaw strain, fair in the five boroughs,
Nordic light pointing-up the Indic raven on the street;
Yellow foam-flecks under the granite step of a waterfall.

Three kinds of curve:
The boar-back ridge, still untilled, lunges frozen;
The River Idle, winding through reed-beds, slow in the flat;
Pap dribbling down the bib of the earth.

Volutes of Coritanian metalwork,
Bedded back in the earth as if in the foundry sand once more.

Three kinds of shelter:
Rabbits in the delved conery, litters tippet each other,
Grass at the door like milk;
Earwigs in the apple's eye, the Riviera of wintering grubs;
And me sleeping in the town amongst my family.

Three more kinds of red:
The fox, sharp-set and brainy, roaming for his living;
Iron case-hardened in an open forge, in the small ironmaster's,
Like skin it changes on warming;
The coke shimmers and swims, neither gravel- nor starling-tint;
Stubble burning off in September, red and black in stripes
Like the furrows of happiness and sadness.

Three kinds of path:
Way of the bird in the air.
Folded winds are pillows of velocity.
He scoops up a song on a hook. One dipped wing
Will tip the world on its edge.
Gallery of the miner in the earth; lead and coal
Strap the stone of thick darkness
Like muscles rigid in some scouring task.
That is a path
Which the eye of the kestrel has not discovered
Nor the foot of the sons of pride.
The eater of the darkness to its rim
Has overturned mountains from the root.
Third
Thought's path in the mapped temples
Fissured like Switzerland.

## Schönheit, Schönheit

The singer cast no shadow, a pool of blackness stirred with him.
You spent all Saturday drinking in the same room, curtains drawn.
Sometimes you can't walk and still no thought breaks free
Of the preventions.
Sometimes the blues have made you starving drunk.

The old star who was afraid of mirrors
Crushed light to a dark metal.
In the bar with the battery-chandelier of spirits bottles, cold shots
Under the lake of green
Where the factory soaks away in the alcohol light
He had to go in and sing
And the night when the music's over
He had to go in and sing
The broken songs and the slurred notes.

He didn't sing but two songs
"I want" and "I'm lost"
Over and over
Over and over
Ten times or more till we broke through.
Then he sang "Please please please".

He was the mirror of desires, of
The greedy heart, of the rooms with the bodies of cans,
The blood in the basin down the hall;
The tenants next door fighting, your words hanging on the air
Unfading, and the years listening after love.
About the way you never grew up,
Adolescence to nothing. You could see through it all.
You saw through it. You lived through it.

The singer was beautiful
In his jacket of leather and steel and fur.
The shadows of his rare gestures

The crying-out slung on a leaden back-beat
Was like the smell of sweat, that food, that stab
The only lyric that doesn't lie.
It was the warmth of a meal made of gin,
The cold of living together seven shifts full time.
He didn't sing out of his throat.

The pink lips and the grey flesh,
The black of a rotting orange around the eyes,
About the veins, even in the temples,
Were love's body, the doll called Pleasure;
And also the real portion:
Under the makeup
Under the stars who fill your evenings
Under the story that replaces memory
Under the fine words
Under the bad luck that's got to turn that wasn't bad luck.
So, the dream lover is out somewhere working all day.
So, you've got high spirits and this is just a bad day.

He sang "I told her, when I kissed your lips
London's twenty thousand streets
And golden San Francisco Bay
Went down in our slipstream."

He sang.
Unable to love, he never gave his love in vain.
He sang about the heart split in two
And overplayed both parts.
He sang the old songs. They'd come true.
The new songs, the ten years of bad ones,
The ones written for money, which made him poor,
And the backing band they paid for
Made it all easy to bear.

# Dhofar

The land got up and was gone,
Strode, rivers flashing and flowing, worms darting like nerve-ends.
This morning we are ten, now we are three.
Last year we were a hundred, now we are a hundred thousand.

We are the guerrillas.
Compared to us, rocks are seen to move
And lightning is slow.
We are the herb which tempts very rare animals to pasture
So that we can turn ourselves into them.
We turn black into green, and dart upwards
But we would prefer to hide beneath the soil!

We speak an idiom that is not Arabic
An idiom of the oppressed, of the mountains, of the gravel seas,
Of the oryx and kestrel.
It is the language of the illiterate,
A language to resist interrogators.
It is a language surpassing all others in beauty
For it acknowledges no rich and poor!
It is a speech like the air, good to breathe.
It is a buckle of brain sense and group action.

Here the rich man has no trachoma or TB, and speaks Arabic.
As for rich, he isn't so much;
Here is no oil, but still foreigners—
Bombardments from the sea. We never saw so much metal.
We have been ruled by slaves, we are in our rising.
We have no history but horses and incense.
Islam never won here. And now socialism.
We learn to read, to conquer the past and the sources of the future.
The British are broken, the Iranians have fled;
The Sultan is a louse in the hair of slaves.

The pastor leads the cow from the byre covered with live grass,
Then he kneels under the irriguous belly and blows, blows,

So that the yielder knows to let the milk down.
Till twenty years ago, we did not know the sea disguised another nation,
We thought we were alone.
Foreigners blew in from the sea like the rare stones from the sky.
This is Ophir, Arabia Felix. Stones with diseased marrows have burnt
      the byre.
After the flail of blindness and the hook of wasting sickness
Here are the mortars, the helicopters, the offshore batteries.

Like the nerve conjoining the quilt of sinew to the shaft of bone
We pierce with information and electricity.
The army taught me how to read and since that time
Thought is different: it has more of myself.
Like worms we'll tread and slough
The ashen, choking sand into a grove of oranges,
We'll drown the fine lady, the pomegranate,
Whose fruit young girls sew onto their robe next to bells,
Into the crumb of the soil.

You occupy the territory, we are it.
We stoop like night hawks in the black fear of our enemies.
We have compassed their foreheads with steel bands,
We have bowed our heads and cut their sinews behind the knee.
One was despair, two was comprehension, three was victory.
Four was the head flush with the stones of the choked watercourse.

Three nations invaded us: Iran, Britain, Saudi Arabia.
On the sea, America. Count only
A hundred and fifty thousand
And you have passed beyond our tongue
And added strangers to our nation.
We will outlast.
We menace like a limestone land sieved by corrosive water.
They will vanish into the generosity of our glorious past.
We will bear them, bier them to their graves.
We will break their metals like threads.
Rocks surge from the earth to bury them.
We are the earth in motion. We are the javelins of the sun.

# Turkish Music

> Lightly holding the purple reins
> We leap to the saddle, our tasselled helmets low,
> Our banners fluttering like crimson clouds,
> Writhing like snakes and dragons in the air.
> Deploying in nine rings we laugh to scorn
> This petty Empire. Can the Hans withstand
> The mighty Tartars?
> As we display our might, the roar of the drums
> Strikes fear into all who hear;
> The bugles sound to form the ranks for battle.
>  —Hong Sheng, *The Palace of Eternal Youth* (1688), scene 16

Midnight has settled on the village square outside,
Where the cattle drive twice a day.
Under my room, in the peasants' house of wood and plaster
Used by the hotel workers
Is the room where the work permit men live out five years,
No family allowed and no respite from the Germans,
To return to Anatolia with the capital.
Time lost, knowledge of death;
Memory lost, narrow and bitter as a knife;
Hearts lost, a gamble of despair
With happiness.
I think of my home but see nothing definite.
I remember the day. Darkness pours in from the snowy forest
And there music is falling from the air.

"At home, the landowners form all sides in parliament,
Control each policy, each wing of the truth.
The man without money is like a wisp of the air
Dressed in old clothes and a skin chapped with too many nerves,
Trying to move against the great wind
Which moans
The breadth of the high steppes.
The poor man trying to move forward out of nothing

Is like the Yuruk, the nomad shepherd blown march by march
Destroying the grass and fleeing
Before a force he cannot name.
Where is he going? he has no rest but his longing,
No earth but his song.
Land is like the taint of race darkening the blood,
Possession is like the rocks: unchangeable.
Peasants are like animals, they cannot own.

We'll irrigate the desert.
We'll give the land to the tiller.

Once the conquerors, horse nomads,
Dealt out the land and broken peoples
To Counts maintaining soldiers, sipahis—
The Army created the State, and the nation was a honeycomb of warriors.
We sowed wheat, harvested ranks of men.
We who were owned, owned nothing.
Nomads, with flocks of men... Today we own nothing
And the rich are not bound to service...

When will I own the farm I served with hand and eye?
When I leave this country
(I have never learnt German)
I will buy a flock of white sheep
I will buy a flock of black sheep
I will buy a grove of lemon trees.
I will raise tomatoes, on that ground more fertile than any other.
I will raise a family to work it.
We will grow enough to eat.
I will buy a share of land, as much as I can till.
No more hunger. But then, the distributors, the buyers..."

They drink and laugh late into the German morning.
We start work at 7.30.
They play electric Turkish music.
It is like the furls

Of molten bronze poured into a cauldron of milk.
It is as if the ashes of night
Shone through with the red grate of stellar fire.
As if the Scorpion, fiery, pinned to the apse of sky,
Arched.
It was like the spasm of my most contorted and strong nerves.
It was like understanding the language of birds.
It was like the taste of copper earth, acrid and binding for ever.
It was the spice of air.
I want to sleep. Instead I listen to this music.
It is as if the waterways of ore within the earth
Belled.

My breath, gasp and heart's heart, is outside me.
I riffle an unskeined pack of memories, heartless shadows.
I have no dwelling in this earth, no possession.
The fields are lonely because they are not English.
I pine for those sensations.
Can you tell me where my country lies?

Does the wind
Turn the dust into birds?
Such are embers of a total song
For whom the earth is nothing but what passes
Hidden in a shriek of wind and blood,
Of passage and ardour.
Song, flown from a far country,
Masonry of the invisible cities,
Architecture of the streets of longing,
Where the singing of women is heard behind barred, fretted windows.
It may be the songs of lovers,
Gay goshawks fluttering against those lattices;
Or the wailing for dead husbands, archaic—
The voice of stone shattering-
Stomach knotted with aloes, resin of sharpness, tight throat;
Agit, barb of frenzy.

Because I know you will never understand my song
Because I know I will never understand this music
Because when you sing, at work,
The heedless song is alien in your throats; because my thoughts are lost in
The distance towards home;

I know beauty is not a form, but affection, a memory
Of your mother, or breath purified in a kiss.
The face in my heart is hard for me to see.
Once we danced and sang in front of men,
Shouting aloud the words we hear when alone.
Exhaustion beat the devils and motion fired our cold clay.
Running in shapes, we left everything behind
And sang in the metre of the triple leap:
triumpe, triumpe, triumpe…
Our dancing days are done. And you drink to forget everything:

"In the Altai mountains,
In Turkestan, in the time of the making of nations
When men were hardly different from soil
The first Turk lived with his sheep and mares.
Our people lived in a valley of brass ringed by an iron mountain.
There was no path through the dark rock
Till we were led to freedom by a grey wolf,
Into the world by a hidden path.
The great steppes were lit by a Sun of blazing iron,
Rare grasses led us over beckoning plains…

Led by a wolf to the slums of the city
We blow through German streets
Like scraps of newspaper
Absorbing dirt
Always empty.

Protect us, great dervish.
We are so many, none can count us
We are so many, none can defeat us

We are so few, no enemy can find us.
We are so many, none can feed us.
We must go to foreigners to ask for rule.
We are sons of the Sun and the whole earth is ours.
We take orders from those who take orders.

Give us
The song in the language in which our names are pure and no longer
        insults,
The air with the Arabian or Balkan flourishes
Like the song used to melt the pain of surgery
In the mountains of the east, where there are few doctors.
There the men sing more strongly than the knife
The song of opium, chant like a second heart
That lets the mind float free in its strength.
Be with us, great dervish. We are so many
None is lonely. None is proud.

We were conquerors, we were slaves.
Will we rise one day when this world ends
Across the bridge of fire and the labouring day
To the space distilling like resin from a slashed tree,
Where the walls of each soul give way
And we are one?"

Up here, I have no music. The melody eludes the tongue.
The lone Puritan voice in the white room
Moves upward from the realm of passions.
We have advanced by severance, deriving thought from loneliness.
The neoterics
Search out archaic words and the unreal past;
And ritualists teach rosaries not knowing what they mean.
Since we have no common and musical speech
Language is reduced to tags of class.
In each image they see a room
And in each room a social rank.

This is a room for kitchen workers to sleep in,
But what we feel is free and up to us.
In the raw night the black storm of music—
You'd think the house poured brandy down a throat of garlic—
Plucks my nerves although my limbs are still.
Pictures run in my head and I am the pictures.
I love this electric music,
Its violence is like the writhe of struggling men, working men.

Each new form is made in the dark
And the old one is like soil buried beneath the earth.
As the millennia of tradition become a basic silence;
When the ornamentation has borne itself down,
And worked itself into a flower with no stem;
When the unspent day is a cruelly stylized space;
I'll remember
Turkish music.

"The drinkers of fermented mares' milk;
The pagans who anointed their Banners with milk in triumph;
The smokers of opium, chasing the heavy fumes
Like the red heart of a black night;
Drink in this landscape of man,
These woods-and-fields of man,
And are pined.

I would like to sit beside the Aegean
Watching the fishing boats drift home at dusk.
I would pour water into the raki,
Which turns cloudy, the colour of lion's milk.
I would eat a lemon, to give it sharpness;
I would eat roast beef, to give it weight.
My family would be there beside me.
I would lack for nothing."

# Builders in Winter

In December cold, I walk home at five
And pass pale figures hanging from a half-there wall.
It's dark. Time to start your own day.
How can they work in this cold?
Hard question. I asked a neighbour:
"We've all got our cross to bear".
Theology in the joints, where the bone sinters,
Fate in the muscles, hard cables and soft crying flesh.
He left the trade, explaining how it crippled you,
But found his way back again.
Liberty till thirty. Afterwards the pains.

How can a frame withstand the winter?
Six months a year, darkness and cold forbid our air,
A tangle of thorns lashing in the steppe of a November sky.
Chilled skin bruises on contact with cold brick
And the workface fades, hard to the eye in the twilight.
Even a young man finds his bones stiff, scale setting in at night;
Frames wired up to bear and they cannot give or shift.
Something like brandy inside them gives heart
And breaks up the veins in their cheeks.
"And if I had my way, and if I listened to my wish,
I'd drink the winter out beside a fire."

The ducal estates still have title to central London,
Rich men make fortunes from empty buildings,
And builders are turned out when the job's done.
Thousands go homeless, or fall ill in damp and squalor
While skilled tradesmen wait on the dole, like waste sites.
You know how manual labour sits in you like an animal,
Inescapable.
Months of college drain it out, leave little else.
A habit of mind firm as the iron cramps inside a wall,
Deep fatigue and unthinkable strength
Are stronger than an athlete,

Shaped and specialized as bone.
If they gave up, the city would collapse.
Pinned to the nails of planned precision,
Each movement is pure geometry translated into thrust…

If you asked, who made the luxury we live in,
The territories, the skylines, the banks, the hollowed spaces,
Each brick was laid by waged men.
Their lives turned to cities, in their works we breathe.

Architect, consider what Irishmen
Made up the gaps in your designs.
Owner, give thanks to what made your titles real.
Cities, you were once an ardour in the chests of men.
It's a grace that I, nesh and clumsy,
Can sit in the lee of winds, in straight-laid walls,
And form the spaces and constructions of my thoughts.

# British Steel

"If this plan is not carried out, in 5 years there will be no British Steel Corporation" —BSC spokesman, 1978

As the reality fades, the dream gathers to a head
Whether among the wolves who dream of what they eat,
The swallows who dream of flight in the wild airs
Or the sheep who dream of nothing
None stands up to be being born an ape.

I love steel.
Before I could talk, there was a smithy in our road;
When I see again flinders curve a red track,
Like thoughts or comets,
Rushing into liquid jewels that grow dark,
Black heart iron transformed under the mouth of spat oxygen
A memory of beauty before my self fills me.
So the riches of the earth reach out into wrought form,
And fire and clay draw out a sheer resplendence.

We were serfs; at the roots of our national strength
Iron and steel tore us from cold, Asian mud.
History run wild burnt the calendar of famine and revolt,
Massacre and religion, birth
And starvation. The cupellation
Purged both ore and men.
Industry was borne on iron machines;
The men from the mills tore down feudalism
As dawn burns down darkness. The fear lifted.
Trade stepped down iron paths, fields
Dug with steel could feed our millions;
Capital, like a vaporised ingot, transformed
Our minds and days. Like water trapped on limestone
Our life collects fruitfully here, pent in.
Steel is the origin of brightness in a
Terrain of wet furrows and smoky cottages.

Steel is the pacer of the will,
The bride of the metallurgical dream.
What a nomad feels for horses,
I feel for steel;
Either sentiment or love of power.
What were we?
We lived, as though under the North Sea,
Under great lords and the gangrenous Church.
What was our motion?
We were not beasts but praying worms.
Civilization blooms in the warmth of foundries,
Our cities are false arcading on steel thrust-lines.
Faith does not exist nor patriotism
But factories give us traction on our greasy lives.
It is the largest shadow thrown on the eye
Which lays the deepest trace in the veins
And wields domination of the shapes within the eye.

Our symbols are technic or agnostic.
The aged fishermen, scholars of the holy texts,
Collectors of debris and cancelled plans,
Turn earth into sand and reveal false omens.
Their academy piles up a papery past.
Clergy with punitive compassion
Praise decline in the pay of the Government.
Truth is a length of cut metal;
Wisdom is the ability to work.
People want homes, and you give them words.

The Titans have scaled heaven,
Their rough voices fracture the discreet coldness.
There's nothing in heaven but more inadequate men,
And their Promethean work was all thrown away.
The agencies of state are beating at the wind
And the owners
Coddled and subsidized from cradle up
Are thieves in the end.

All our manufacturing industry is threatened,
And all it brings: a civil order.
We are approaching the 18th century.
As the reality fades, the dream draws to a head.

# Britanskaya SSR

Russia, who'd have thought it?
Their inert, immense, novels, trackless tundras of prose-
Like monumental barracks, that crush the eye in its course-
Bury the ego under ice.
No flicker of wit, none of worldly desire
Hampers the souls' desire to obey
And the Khan's desire to command.

Worship of ignorance, contempt for this life.
Are persuasive. The self grows weary of its capers,
The exterior machine cannot grow weary. One wins,
And makes the water dead. We could be
Drunk-intoxicated, or drunk-cleared down,
Erasing ourselves as we wait for order;
Reeling or paralysed-stiff.

There, art promotes obedience, and fun is neat vodka:
The taste of nothing and the vehicle to nothing.
The blurred fragments of a late Hellenism
Wander in rags beside the freezing Tanais.

They rule the Tadzhiks, and why not the British?
They rule the Poles, and why not the French?
They rule themselves. And that makes me truly afraid.
They make the clever more stupid than the simple dolt,
Who is more stupid than the public corpses;
For spectacle, they watch their neighbour buckled by a whip
And strain in emulation of inner abnegation.

When the twin states, Wehrmacht and Red Army,
Held the continent down like a cow being flayed,
From Finnmark to Crete and from Ural to Finisterre,
They fought over Western civilization.
If that flower of romance existed,
Its heroes would have acted nobly.

What do they bring us as they pursue freedom,
*Za svobodu*, while she still can get away;
How far can she lead them?

Greek corrupted by woodsmen,
And peasants rounded up by the Mongol herdsman.
No trace remains of Perun, the Oak, or the Moist Earth Mother,
Of Aryan culture,
Of the famous free, landholding peasants.
Designs still used in embroidery
Might be Khor, the sun, but no-one really knows.
The men who did the effacing
Have their eyes on us. What then?
The Church of Iron; control systems and State TV; Pavlov's liturgy.
Another wall, another poster girl. The same factory.
Advertising or agitprop feminise the masonry.
Pick up your heap of dust and eat it.
Your quota of appetite, and of finished units.
You drool yourself some story; because truth eats the self.
I inhale Brecht, Neruda, Gramsci; not
Because they tell the truth but because they deceive
Totally, totally
Over and over and over and over.
I'd like to see my bosses shot.

In the book of the Prophet
The end of the time of oppression is announced,
And the instrumentality of the same.
Might shall destroy itself by excess,
Righteousness is found
Within the teeth of the world-power, the 4th Monarchy.
You, who have lost the world,
Let it pass. Release your sway.
You shall give it up and find the Kingdom.
We look into the paced-out emptiness
We number our condition under the laws of Man
And the wind of perfection blows the numbers away.

Good men do nothing
They open the eye of the mind
And the high slanting walls vanish.
We survey our justice and forget it. All crimes are paid.
The 5th Monarchy is the beast whose hooves shall break
The very ground it stamps on. There is an end of ends and changes.

In the interior, full of streams like white severed tongues,
Are Aztec mines in the Transbaikal; there is
Metal, the ultimate reason of state; a continent
Of solid money. Oh those Empires of unbroken soil
Were no signs have been cut into the earth
And where the bird of ice holds gold in its claws.
A hill made of iron at Magnitogorsk,
Gas, uranium, oil.
Wheat sleeps in the virgin earth
And primary peoples wait to be exploited.
There is the balance of Europe's future-the balance-and the wares!

Russia. Who'd have thought it?
Nu, it could have been the Germans.

# Lusitanian Angel

Lusitanian Angel, songbird of the wind and of forms
Your words build their cities on unpeopled waters
Phoenician cargoes put in at the great wharves—
Pinnacles uphold the palazzi
Pirates come home to die in the docklands
Then you draw round the magic plough that calls walls home to earth,
Wipe them out with birds and forests that rush towards the light,
Create the race that wanders in the forests, led by woodpeckers,
And tells stories of the vanished towers,
Epics, ballads, folktales, floorplans, children's rhymes.
And vanishes in final proof of this.
And here is the water, still unpeopled.

Life is a series of novels
Characters like Venetian blinds' light-flecks
Made of water, washing-machines, warm blankets, petrol on puddles,
Words like smoke, tingeing the light,
Fumetti.
The heroine changes her name and then her hair and then her face.
In Chapter one she organizes Cells, in her tight-fitting overalls,
She only likes to work.
In Chapter Two she has a fit of the torpids and becomes a white doe rabbit.
In Chapter Three she is the grass on the roof of the modern hotel
At the back where it becomes a hill.
In chapter Four she's Irma Vep, a dashing jewel thief
Leaping off roofs
And dancing in cafés.
In Chapter Five she's on the radio singing 'Heartful of Soul' in a voice like
    lipstick
Draw the curtains and say goodbye to the real.
In Chapter 243 she's rainwater landing on an illuminated sign and
    evaporating.
Is she sincere?
She says things to me which she'd already said
To my friend Osmond

Reading while fishing in Lincolnshire
In 1974.
But then, what she said to our old English teacher…
What is consciousness but imaginary conversations?
What is conversation but assimilation or dissimilation?
The room rushes away like frames of cinema reel and towards you.
The wall normally isn't seen but now the shadow of an unreal girl
Invents it, a silhouette falling wind-swayed onto the plaster.
I am absolutely free to become Ossian or Xerxes.
The face in the mirror is ice-still and what moves across my eyes
Is me. Today, Slob Connard, who I am drinking Chinese gin with.

Pessoa, born in Durban, son of Empire,
Wrote two volumes in English.
Later, he published poems under three different names,
In three different styles, swathed in fictive biographies.
Poets need biographies, but it's more modern to make them up.
Events are chance,
My fantasies are sincere and profound.
Events are just things you couldn't prevent.
The intrinsic rhythm of his tenoned personalities
Rode on a very high level of language:
You master the phonemes, master the formatives, master the I rules,.
By cutting all the threads except one
We manufacture personality, faking the log-book
Stop your pretending. Cast off the moorings.
What's inevitable is the elimination and Self
Is the face on the cutting-room floor.
In the triple space of the three projections
Cast on an expansive darkness
He composed his inner face like a gilt, basilicate, ballroom.
Kipling believed
Stories were possessing spirits, messages from Outside,
Beyond the personality. He was not Pessoa.
Definitely not. Well, perhaps a little bit.
Whatever the machine prints out
Is more than it can take in.

My poetry is not my self.
I existed before English, but my poetry is made out of:
Conversation, class impacts, and fashion raised to rules.
I locate my essence in details:
I am made out of apples, surfaces, payslips, cheques,
Fabrics, a hairdresser's weaknesses.
This is my attitude
To attitudes.

You don't hear the words but the man that's behind them;
The millions of data
Reduced to human gestures.
Though every fact in Rostovtzeff were obsolete or bent,
I still repass every moment of my life in one evening with him.
His fantasy sticks, and the facts disappear.
The shape of history is all in the composing mind.
Kings and queens are functions of narrative,
Heroes are unreal figures in theoretical space.
Just as thoughts are the sluice of blood-barged nutrients
So an idea is just a nerve of an ardent glance.

At the maximum of my aspirations
When the moon is out;
When my spirits, drunk on fumes, run like storms;
When I say, enough of the old life!
When the greatness of the world, which frightens me,
Is the magnitude dissolved in my eyes
No larger than a bud;
When my egoism is like a machine and like a Convent girl,
The marble head of Virgil appears in my room
And the lonely, drunken, Pessoa.

He wanted to be the pimp of the city to itself
Of the night shift clattering down some street as the poet stumbles home
Of daylight rats, faster at 13 than schoolkids ever,
Of lying smoking in hotels with running walls,
Of shopgirls, waitresses, smart receptionists,

Of gangsters in the mayor's palace and
Grafters aiming to replace their bosses;
Of knurls, gangue, splines, bezels, flanges,
Of speeches by the president on the radio,
As formal as poetry;
Of the boy out in the brickfield with his bottle of wine,
Of the wallpaper on the shorn wall of half-demolished buildings.
I wish I was
The pusher of images, with red pupils and diamonds for my dog-teeth
I'd stand in Greek Street giving aesthetes the connection.
I'd have phials of Arcadia and blotting-paper soaked in Red Dawn.

I love Portugal, where I have never been.
In her revolution I purify my heart,
In its songs, theses, posters, laws, debates, etc.
And I love Pessoa.

I am not Fernando Pessoa
But Fernando Pessoa could be me.

## 'Laughing Man': self-portrait by Richard Gerstl

The laugh is a black pulse out, blackout,
It smells the heretic's pyre.

The air is flayed,
It gashes in a livid, greenish, throttle.
Membranes are choked with a gulp of combusting gas.
His face is a red devil-mask of wood the peasants wear
(Draped and masked we go down the mountainside towards the village
Bounding and leaping)
His rictus gasps in the world like a white flame of Alpine air.

Artistic forms burn up in a cyclonic opiate rush
Nerves pour back from the head to the entrails, the crawlers
The self-portrait is a skin above a mask
Consumptive slum-girls strike the noble classical poses
The marble effigies in the royal staterooms
Cover each other in red booths as small as ovens

He laughs at the years of labour like coma
Real experience slips through the blocks of habit like a thief
Work? what was that?
Instinct is an old dog and intelligence is lethal.
He laughs
Like a man throwing up the intoxication of life
And passing out.
"I am God, I made this caricature."

Laughing, the eyes of buildings go black—
Diaphragms taut, bellowing, ripped—
The images in their windows crack,
Their bones are carious.

The lizards in the formal gardens are marked with laughing heads.
The dressed stone turns to the soft animal beneath it.

When such a man laughs
Paper shares are worth no more than what a painter scrawls on
Brokers drink themselves into a coma
Money grows sick and whirls like fever dreams
The Palace of Justice burns, and the book of land deeds with it
The expression of the double eagles
Unfurled to fly through Serbia or the Kirghiz Steppe
Twists until it is his.

# Engineer Grade II

Invisible smog of stupidity and greed!
Hundreds of engineers, jangling nylon carpets,
Miles of white sepulchral Modern Style façades
Malevolent gnomes from Coventry on the phone
Propagating plants, smoky black workshops
Signs saying Internal Vacancy and Terminal Room
Inky fingers, inky thoughts
Beautiful Chinese women from the Red Chamber Dream
Tall as Mongols, stroll by but are in other departments
Old bureaucrats more disgusting than punks work with me
Files, all connecting files withdrawn or liquidated

3 o'clock. My afternoon drifts by like wading through treacle standing
    on your head
Johnny Malrousseau rings. He had to get my number from the New York
    office.
I try to tell him about IBM and the payroll software.
More and more songs about washing machines and underpasses.
"I was writing about walls and machines before anybody else"
"Only old wave stars write about living in foreign hotels."
"Angst in expensive decor, set against a snowy forest,
A cross between Edmund Goulding and Patrick Modiano. Ha!"

"But, don't you want a good time?
People could be watching Olivia Newton-John
And you come on like a zombie with a German accent
Don't you want to be loved?"
"Pain is just the memory of a higher future or a severed past."

We trail cultural assets, ATV, Cabaret Voltaire,
In an attempt on complicity, drowning
In books and films and record company lobbies
Where he hustles for tickets and records.
We're too intelligent to see through it
And too competitive to impress each other.

"People want a song about someone more expensive than they are
Better spoken, too,
Crying tears of kir or Burgundy
Into a very good-looking mirror.
That's the uplift, the diagonal, the catnip."
"That's OK. I've got more soul than them
Because I've got more vanity."
"What do you do in your factory?"
"The same as Greta Garbo in *Ninochka*. You know—planirovaniye."

4 o'clock. The walls read like a C.P. Snow novel.
The minutes don't unwind, they have come off the bobbin.
I have to go back to coil the tape.
Five o'clock. Six thousand of us stream out of the works gates
Like the untuned despairs of an impure poet.
I camouflage as a human being and go down to the ICA.
The curving, metal, smooth, swishing subterraneans
Are the snakes in the Gardens of the Hesperides
The Western Paradise where the blessed dead are ferried
(By Frisians; I'm a Frisian of philology and dialectic);
Above in the orchard, are the guardians.
The capitalist sirens of Vogue allure;
The ultrawaitresses of Lord Leighton are Grand Verticals;
Preraph felines, full of mouse or mysticism, arch their backs.
I copy down the walls for use in poems.

The sun, commuter from Cimmeria to Avalon,
Folds up his brass plate and dons gleaming leathers,
The sky, in an onrush of pathic sentimentality,
Has turned into a vast unrolling bolt of wine.
The Serpentine, turned to Calvados, composes the shadowy faces of Eve
    and Lilith
Out of Trafalgar Square, under Admiralty Arch, into the Mall.
In the ICA theatre, the latest in an endless series of
Agitprop bands from the Manchester area
Harrow the hell of their London audience.
In the gallery next door

A private showing of pictures for the Queen's collection.
Red Guards ride past, black dog's heads dangling from their saddlebows,
They fretfully massacre stray punks

Music from the offal in the prolos' chests
Flashes and screams among the paradise of dainty devices
Student nurses are pharmacornucopias and rhythm is realistic
Pornography
Blooms of virtù say, nature has no viscera
Change is in the past
Which was always really the same anyway
We have fine skins. We are going to keep it that way.
Trivialised history: the residue and material of history
The faecal fetishes of centuries turned to stasis:
The live art we are afraid to touch the radical life.
The Pharisees: Babylon.
The waste of the balanced, optimised probabilities
Kids who get beaten up by the police for the way they dress
The owners of the law
The burning masses who convert my art from babbling schizophrenia

The comptrollers of the grants I want to live on.
I'm just a pimp of images, a vehicle for cargoes I can't control.
What produces consciousness
The amount of suffering you do in a day
Or the amount of money you own?

Back home in the factory
I realise the nervous system is a bureaucracy
The Recording Angel is a peasant of the ledger
Whimpering for the neobarbs to come in and burn the books.
My subconscious fails to invite me to essential meetings
I have to bribe a monkey to get food
The infrastructure is run by a guild of rats
The office makes them vegetate, at night they're on night-rate.
Mystery trains roll into the undarkened midnight
Train, train.

A thought is a 3 microsecond logic gate
The chain of precedents is a chain of gates
Every century of culture means another year's school
The calendar is a Chaldaean zodiac
And the ravelled sleeve of time
Is a protocol of dropped stitches.
The specification is in Egyptian and the maintenance modules are
Cuneiform cylinders
30,000 sheets of documentation per subsystem
The membranes are all covered in Syriac and
The interfaces are blown personae.
Grim senior secretaries refuse to give me a new pencil
The junior secretaries are mouths of shadow.
Short scarred men rush in and out
"Synergy! Synergy!" they cry and fall into taxis.

The eel down my back is the Tower of Babel. Babylon doth fall.
Somewhere in the geniza is my lost, smiling, heart.
I am surrounded by fish turned human.
I am a wasps' nest, each leaf stamped with the face of
Lady Subtly Accelerating Mare...

# In the Red Grove

The beautiful Chinese at the computer terminal has notes in ideograms

The bit stream remanifests itself as machine code in Hertfordshire

Similar bit-streams migrate as winged beetles or pause as mushrooms

The reworked Hell's Angel dallies down the road
Brass valves were removed from his head
(Through the brainstem and yanked out through the clavicle)
Recast in an open forge in a country famous for clean air
Left in a February dyke for three weeks
Chafed down with worn high-denier silk stockings
Tuned to a mellow gong frequency, and refitted.
His aggressions were deterged with grit-guns, like old colleges.
His subliminal dramas were played out at the Essoldo (In the mornings)
His damp course, above the first vertebra, was relaid.
He used to go Paki-bashing: now he teaches housewives yoga.
His jacket now speaks in gleaming steel studs:

Georg Groddeck. Ferenc Juhász. Max Ernst.

In Golders Green the greatest living expert on the Babylonian Talmud
Has an epiphany of numbers while passing the old pink theatre.
The true and false zodiac, the Cabbala, the Messiahs,
The twelve months of the year, the twelve tribes, and the 13th, secret,
      moon
Are mapped on the stucco as if with an aerosol and stencil.

It looks something like a rosy cricket pitch
Or a screen with plotter stitched into the stucco
Later, he uses a map of London for gematria.
He knows: the number of great poems written in a century
The numbers scattered on the breeze in isobars
The numbers memorised by Miriam or Yehudi
The numbers stacked in the depository, baled and corded

A blueprint stored in numbers waiting for men with their decoding arms
The number of Urs you can touch in your life
The number of sparks in a great poem,
The system behind London bus numbers
The efficiency of manweeks (roughly 0.76)

The number of serious possibilities
Herwarth's treatise on the accuracy of statistics
Eteomathematics, treated entirely without axioms
The skeins of wool you can gather on a wet morning
The numbers in the nervous system
(Like the statistical charts of Le Roy Ladurie
The mass observation of consciousness)
The angle of what's heard to what's meant,
The absolute tempo of perception, the score as written,
He has traffic tables for each date and notion,
The quantity of thought: pitch, calibre, tessitura, erlangs, kilohertz,
    presence, soul.

What is the Red Grove?
It is the inner environment considered as a copse.
Where a pram rusts, woodlice snuggle inside the lining.
The red grove is by Woodhouse Eaves
That is, the Eaves of the forest.
Rooks, not housemartins. In the Wood House
Tapestries moulder. In the decaying mansion of chaffinch and crayfish
Ancestors have walks of life, not portraits.
Antlers are heirlooms of silver laid down in velvet preservers,
The trees change dresses for each season—
Near-naked in the winter Riviera,
Their confections yield froissements in the summer winds.
Small leaves, caught on masses of spiders' webs,
Are patterns of cards
In the smoking-room where gentlemen gamble.
Heritable wealth plummets to the working, barmy mould.
Trees are great estates, cut up and mulched
By solicitor-worms and bark-beetles.

In the Red Spinney
Shuttles weave, controlled by cards,
Heckled by babies glossolalling,
This napery stitched with Quarlesian emblems
Antimacassars of polite diction
Dyed with kermes and spilt wine
Sheets made from nocturnal rivers
Doilies of metonymy primping the unsayable, also negative doilies
Camouflage-tunics of sublimation and cheerful bouncing ignorance
Tramp-nightgear of mediaeval Greek manuscripts
Teacosies showing "The Poet's head in the throes of inspiration"
Veils for the virgin shattered by the nuptial trances of flowers
Handpainted ties for spivs showing the Muse sunbathing
Smocks with live, moving pictures of the internal juicescape
Albs showing faithful maps of fields: clover, couchgrass, bumps
Which textual scholars memorize for use in exams
Pelisses of bee-fur and sweet-chestnut pods, and mares' tails—
And they tear them down each night in the sleepgrove.

What is a red grove?
The modern Herrick; the Jungian missal;
The telex receiver without wires,
Reading seeds, feathers, psychoactive ions, throw of smokestacks;
The issuer of books printed on wasps' nests;
Alcoholic of the sweet juices in nettle flowers;
The Boswell of mould growing on cheeses;
The self-awareness of cuckoo-spit.

# The Poet and the Schizophrenic

We both have voices inside
You can't understand yours
Mine speaks the natural language of the human soul.

You can't work because you can't adapt because you are asocial.
I have Weltschmerz and mal du siècle.

You hit on a vein to make the blood come.
I inhale inspiration.

You'll be post-mad. Light work and anti-depressants.
I'll be a literary critic. I envy you.

You have a doctor to listen to you sometimes.
I sue to the NHS for an audience.

We both have private worlds.
You're a hunted animal in yours.
I'm a king in mine. Dead poets live there.

You sit in a room and the room screams.
I sit in a room and tell the walls to show some affection.

I am rapt.
You don't move around much.

You are regressive.
I concentrate, and return to the Golden Age of matter.

You look at a wall and see the cemented grid of your unhappiness.
I look at a wall and see a white, peeled, wand
Then I see a tree half ablaze and half in flower
Which becomes a forest whose thoughts are birds, birds...

You were made by your family background, or by some virus.
I became when I saw the moon in the bare trees.
You imagine a dream lover you can't imagine—
Who would be ideal for you wouldn't be best suited.
I sing a lyric call to anyone who ever looked beyond the world
Anyone of the regressive literary intelligentsia
Anyone at all.

We both operate in metonymy.
You dip your language in the loss so no-one can understand
I work in colours of the light of happiness.

You move through a landscape peeled of expectations
Where houses are not shelter and riches are not calm.
I am post-modern.

No-one understands what you say because you're worthless.
No-one understands what I say

I'm above you.
You're inside me like the sacrifice inside a god.

# Dead Wind

Storm winds scour the streets of the winter town.
Rags stir in an alley,
Eddies of grit blow in my eyes.
A scree of dust blows up the neck of the streets
Like shale down an empty stream bed.
Rubbish is thrown up on waste lots,
Bright colours of dead manufactures.
Odours wash from dumps and incinerators:
The pyres of carcasses which part flesh and bone.

Poor youths shelter between close walls,
Like sheep in a hollow on the moor.
They live out on the street and beg; high above
I stare out into the wind zone,
Flesh numbed in the flagrance of the idiot wind,
In the immunity. I listen to music.
My destiny written on torn scraps of paper
Goes round and round in the street, numb terrain.
A wind blows from the dead heart of things.
A vain liquid pulses in the canals of my ear,
Dead wind.

The streets are full of lies and fears and powers.
Intimate poses smile from posters, the frozen
Flesh blown up covers the side of buildings,
The drilling of images wearies the eye.
No-one looks at each other: broken gazes broken words.
Our assent creates huge chaussées,
Scoured by inhuman forces.
The cars crawl by like a reel of film in coma,
Grit roar and fumes waft up on a metal wind.
Commerce corrupts dead sense. The air is soaked in words…
Shapes in my mind buckle and taint, realigned
By null forces.
A sick wind creases the sky
A sick wind jars the words in my mouth.

Numbers, numbers
The tangent to the curve of change veers over,
The body of oppression bursts, its parts shift shape.
The axis starts to spin
The pure light falls on the pure lens
Material factors reverse their moments
The axis drives
The cup of bitterness is broken, the winged seeds
Plunge into the bridal earth. All movements
Find their end. How many more years?

Stone is winnowed on the threshing-floor of winds.
Vague cries from the death of matter.
The supple riddle sifts a grain of stone.
Tall buildings are ruined incessantly;
The edifice of thought shivers instantly.
Time swathes cities like a man walking through reeds.
A celestial jaw polishes the brick-husks into dust.
Verticality is laid low,
The hedges of struts cannot resist. The term
Of their arcs is ruin. Ruins of Time
Are the fauna of memory: living stones.
Stone reared up is the properties of the City,
Stone crumbled is the flesh of the black earth.
The living eye has read the scriptures to the end.

Your voice is torn away.
I see mouths rent open without a sound
I cannot catch the words.
A rat riddles the walls and substructures
A jackal slinks
Along the lines of towering graves.
Through broken windows and into deserted rooms
An oracle wind gasps out, in the dry skull of the City,
"How many more years?"
A dead wind drains the warmth from my head.
A sick wind drains the words in my mouth.

www.ingramcontent.com/pod-product-compliance
Lightning Source LLC
Chambersburg PA
CBHW031148160426
43193CB00008B/298